Music Teachers' Values and Beliefs

In *Music Teachers' Values and Beliefs*, Dwyer investigates the relationships between teachers, learners and music in music classrooms. Using Bourdieu's concepts of habitus and doxa as an interpretive lens, the book explores the values and beliefs of four music teachers, depicted in richly detailed narratives. The narratives are contextualized through the examination of traditions of music and contemporary approaches. In the past, music education has been shaped by elitist tendencies regarding the types of music worthy of study, the ways in which music should be learnt, and the purpose of such learning. Contemporary approaches to music education have enacted significant change in some regions and systems, while others have been slower to leave behind deeply entrenched values, beliefs and practices. These approaches have been blamed for low rates of participation and engagement in school music education, despite the fact that the majority of young people listen to and enjoy music outside of school. This innovative book provides music education researchers and practitioners with a new understanding of the impact of teachers' personal values, beliefs and experiences of music and music education on classroom practice, and the impact this has on students' experiences of music education.

Rachael Dwyer is a musician, teacher and researcher, with her interests including music teacher education, sociology of music education, research education and narrative inquiry. She spent a number of years as a music specialist teacher in primary and secondary schools prior to completing her doctoral studies at the University of Queensland, Australia. Rachael's doctoral research sought to investigate how music teachers' values and beliefs about music and music education are enacted in practice and how these beliefs are socially and culturally shaped. Rachael is currently a research fellow at The Queensland Conservatorium, Griffith University.

Music Teachers' Values and Beliefs

Stories from music classrooms

Rachael Dwyer

Routledge
Taylor & Francis Group

LONDON AND NEW YORK

First published 2016 by Routledge

2 Park Square, Milton Park, Abingdon, Oxfordshire OX14 4RN
52 Vanderbilt Avenue, New York, NY 10017

Routledge is an imprint of the Taylor & Francis Group, an informa business

First issued in paperback 2019

British Library Cataloguing in Publication Data
A catalogue record for this book is available from the British Library

Library of Congress Cataloguing in Publication Data
A catalog record for this book has been requested

ISBN: 978-1-4724-5814-8 (hbk)
ISBN: 978-0-367-22932-0 (pbk)

Typeset in Times New Roman
by Out of House Publishing

To my advisers and mentors:
Professor Margaret Barrett
For expecting more from me than I ever thought I could give, my work would not be what it is without your guidance

Professor Scott Harrison
Whose unwavering support was integral as this work made its transition from dissertation to book

To my participants:
Michael Cook, Sam Hall, Jan Laws and Jayden Wood
For their generous donation of time and energy, despite having little of either to spare

To my family and supporters:
My husband, Bradley Dwyer
Without whom, I never would have written a word

My father, Brian King
1953–2011
For his unquestioning support of my impractical pursuits

My mother and sisters, Kay King, Melanie Neilson and Angela Cummings
For always caring about me far more than you ever cared about my work

My 'cheerleaders'
Too many to name, the research students and academics whose words made me believe I could continue when I was ready to give up

Contents

1 Introduction   1

   Interlude: narrative beginnings   10

PART I
Framing the narratives   13

2 Bourdieu's theory of practice   15

3 The field of music education   21

4 The habitus of a music teacher   30

PART II
The narratives   37

5 Michael Cook at St Mark's College   43

6 Sam Hall at Chiswick College   63

7 Jan Laws at Blackfield State High School   88

8 Jayden Wood at Seaview State High School   111

PART III
Narratives illuminated   131

9 Capital, habitus and field in music education:
   hierarchies, traditions and marginalisation   133

   References   145
   Index   153

1 Introduction

This book is about school music teachers' values and beliefs, and how these shape students' experiences of music education. It explores how music teachers' values and beliefs are shaped by their own experiences of education and their interactions in musical fields, which, in turn, shape the way music curricula are interpreted and enacted. The book explores the way values, beliefs, dispositions and assumptions are socially and culturally acquired. They shape the way we see the world, and are shaped by our early upbringing, our participation in particular social groups and communities.

One of the reasons this is particularly important for school music education is because music teachers invariably have a different experience of music education from that of the majority of the students they teach. Those pursuing tertiary study in a music-related field will have experienced some level of success in music learning, and in schooling more broadly. As is the case with other specialist disciplines, music teachers develop strong beliefs about what musical knowledge and skills are valuable to their students (Richardson, 1996), most often aligning with what was emphasised in their own music education. This, of course, leads to tensions when the students' desires for musical learning differ from the teachers'.

The existing literature on music teachers' values and beliefs, and the ways in which they are enacted in practice, seems to suggest three basic premises about music teachers. First, that music teachers' values and beliefs are shaped by their musical socialisation, which is most often within the sphere of Western art music. Second, that this contributes to a propensity for music teachers to treat their students as if they are preparing them for tertiary music studies, teaching them as if they were future professional musicians. Third, that these values, beliefs and practices are exclusionary and inappropriate. These ideas will be discussed in turn, before describing the ways that they shaped the research study on which this book is based.

Talent, elitism and hierarchy in Western music making

Music making in Western societies is informed by the belief that participating in music is reserved for those with innate talent[1] (Merriam, 1964; Messenger,

1958; Nettl, 1989; Small, 1977, 1998). This is a deeply ingrained social belief that is rarely questioned (Koza, 2001); despite the fact that research has shown that expert performance is a result of deliberate practice (Ericsson, 2006; Lehmann and Ericsson, 1997). Further, ethnomusicological research has shown that all-inclusive, communal music making is the norm in many non-Western cultures (Blacking, 1973, Merriam, 1964, 1967). The majority of adults in Western countries label themselves as 'unmusical', convinced that their relationship with music should be as a consumer. As Small (1998) says, 'our powers of making music for ourselves have been hijacked ... while a few stars, and their handlers, grow rich and famous through selling us what we have been led to believe we lack' (p. 8). This has led to a shift in the way music is conceptualised within Western cultures to that of a consumable, something to be bought and sold rather than something that people do (Small, 1998). Possession of talent is a means of hierarchisation of participation in music making, with those who are 'able' to sing or play being applauded, and those who compose, revered.

In addition to a hierarchy of activities, there exists a hierarchy of musical styles, based on ways in which value systems of individual musical styles intersect with broader values about art and cultural production. As will be explained more fully in Chapters 2 and 3, each musical style has knowledge, skills and attributes that are considered valuable, along with guiding principles about what the music is for. If we compare Western art music and jazz (speaking in broad generalisations), there are differences between the importance placed on the musicianship skills of reading notation and improvising. However, there are similarities between the two styles in terms of the emphasis placed on economic gain, with artistry most often prioritised over financial success. Those who invert these two priorities are branded 'sell-outs'. If we compare these two styles with commercial popular music, musicianship and artistry are often secondary to the economic motivations.

Music teachers' socialisation

Music teacher candidates most often have a background in Western art music (Bouij, 2004, Bowman, 2007, Hargreaves *et al.*, 2007, Regelski, 1997, Ross, 1995); as Philpott (2010) identifies, it is difficult for people without such training to become music teachers at all. It makes sense that teachers who are immersed in this musical culture take the ideas with them into the music classroom. Their identity as a music teacher is formed within it, and it is inevitable that the views they inherit will shape their work as teachers (Hargreaves *et al.*, 2007).

In particular, the literature identifies a number of values with roots in the Western art music tradition that influence music teachers' practice. The reverence for 'the canon' and, by association, dead, white, male composers (Bradley, 2007; 2012; Gould, 2012) presents particular ideas about who music education, particularly composing, is for. Pedagogy has been shaped by conservatism, which has stifled innovation (Philpott, 2010), as has the development of methods and curricula that seek to control (Benedict, 2009). Efforts to challenge or displace these ideas in music teacher education have typically involved the 'bolting-on' of additional experiences (Philpott, 2010) in popular musics, non-Western musics and informal pedagogies, which, unsurprisingly, have not resulted in widespread change. As research in teacher education more broadly has found, values and beliefs are highly durable, with change being difficult (Tillema and Knoll, 1997) and, where it does occur, usually superficial and/or temporary (Cochran-Smith, 1991; Mills 2012).

Music education as elitist and exclusionary

As many have identified, there is potential for music teachers' values and beliefs about music, based on their own experiences of music and music education, to lead to exclusionary practices (Koza, 2001; Regelski, 1997, 2012). Music in secondary schools has a low uptake rate among students at the senior level when compared with other arts forms (Bray, 2009; Lamont, Hargreaves, Marshall, and Tarrant, 2003; Lamont and Maton, 2010; Mills, 1996). School music is considered, at best, to fail to connect music making at school with students' out-of-school musical worlds (Allsup, 2010; Lamont *et al.*, 2003), and, at worst, to tacitly or overtly exclude students with limited knowledge, skill, experience and interest in the teachers' favoured styles of music (Mills, 1996; Regelski, 2012; Ross, 1995).

As Green (2008) identifies, both the content – the knowledge and skills, and the repertoire used to teach them – and the pedagogy of music education have held to longstanding traditions. Western art music is positioned as a superior style in some music education programmes, not only through its prominent place in the curriculum, but through the replication of its values and practices in the classroom. This may lead to students seeing music education as 'not for the likes of me', even in the absence of an explicit indication that this is the case.

There are signs that the landscape of music education is changing, or at the very least, recognition of the ways in which music education needs to change in order to become more inclusive and more relevant to the lives of young people. There are a number of authors critiquing the ways in which practices of music education promote ideas of exclusivity, and suggesting ways that things might be done differently (Bernard, 2004, Bowman, 2007a, 2007b; Bradley, 2006, 2007; Regelski, 1998; Schmidt, 2005; Väkevä, 2006; Väkevä and Westerlund, 2007; Vaugeois, 2007; Westerlund, 2006; Wright, 2008). While further work still needs to be done, the increasing interest in informal music learning (Green, 2002, 2008; Karlsen and Väkevä, 2012) provides examples of how music education might deviate from traditional pathways, providing experiences that are inclusive and responsive to students' needs.

Conducting the research

In response to the issues identified in the literature, this study sought to investigate secondary classroom music teachers' values and beliefs. Three overarching questions guided the inquiry:

- What values and beliefs do music teachers hold about music, music-making and music teaching and learning?
- How are these values and beliefs shaped by institutions and traditions of music, music education and schooling?
- How are these values and beliefs enacted in pedagogy and curriculum?

In order to interrogate these ideas, the study took the form of a narrative inquiry with four music teacher participants in different schools.[2] In each school site, the data generation included formal interviews with the teacher, school principal and a small number of students, informal conversations, classroom observations and artefact analysis. The fieldwork was completed in Queensland, Australia between March 2009 and November 2010, with ethical clearance granted by The University of Queensland, School of Music.

Semi-structured and open-ended interviews were used. The interview schedules were used as a guide rather than a script for the interviewer. The actual questions and the order in which they were asked varied between participants. Each of the student participants and school principals was interviewed once. Each of the teachers was interviewed twice: once prior to or early in the observations and once following the observations. The follow-up questions in the post-observation interview allowed for expansion, elaboration and revision of the views and opinions expressed in the initial interview, and these interviews were much more open-ended in structure.

In addition to the interviews, observations were conducted as a way of enriching the data. The data gathered during the observations in the classroom and school settings provided a context for the interview data, but also drew attention to examples of tensions between the teachers' values, beliefs and practices that could not have been explored through interview alone. The equivalent of four to five days was spent in each school, although this was in most cases a series of partial days spread over two to three weeks in order to maximise the observation of the teacher working in the classroom. Each visit was documented with field notes, which varied from a list of the activities in a particular lesson, to drafts of narrative vignettes recording the classroom happenings. The observations were largely unstructured in nature: I entered each field setting with no predetermined list of events and behaviours to observe that were any more specific than the phenomena embedded in the research questions.

Narrative inquiry

Narrative inquiry is an epistemological approach to research through which the knowledge of people's lived experience is explored and interrogated.

(Clandinin and Connelly 2000; Connelly and Clandinin, 2006) suggest that 'narrative inquiry comes out of a view of human experience in which humans, individually and socially, lead storied lives' (Connelly and Clandinin, 2006, p. 477). Pinnegar and Daynes (2007) claim that narrative inquiry is characterised by a shift away from the traditional relationship between the researcher and the researched. Clandinin and Connelly (Clandinin, 2010; Clandinin and Connelly, 2000; Connelly and Clandinin, 2006) claim that this is what distinguishes narrative inquiry from other forms of research.

> By coming alongside, over time and in relationship, we are able to name, to show, to talk about, to dwell in the tensionality and to learn from the experiences of dwelling within.
>
> (Clandinin, 2010, p. 9)

As Barrett and Stauffer (2009) identify, living alongside participants and drawing upon that experience of living as a source of data is a deeply relational research process, resulting in a co-construction of the research data. Opportunities to revisit the data – to relive and retell, and to discuss the events in more depth – allow for deeper levels of negotiation and interpretation of the data. This process of negotiation is central to narrative inquiry, casting the participants in a more collaborative role in the research process. Ollerenshaw and Creswell (2002) suggest that 'collaboration involves negotiating the relationships between the researcher and the participant to lessen the potential gap between the narrative told and the narrative reported' (p. 332). In the narratives presented in this book, the recursive approach to data generation and the ongoing negotiation of the text resulted in the detection of changes in the teacher's beliefs about music teaching and his students that would not have been evident in a 'snapshot'-like research approach.

Data were analysed using Polkinghorne's (1995) conceptualisation of narrative analysis. Data is analysed by developing or discovering 'a plot that displays the linkage among the data elements as parts of an unfolding temporal development' (p. 15). As Polkinghorne articulates, narrative analysis is actually more aptly described as a method of synthesis, whereby events and happenings (the data) are constructed into a coherent whole that seeks to illustrate a particular phenomenon or how a particular situation came to be. Events, happenings, interactions and conversations that illustrate this were synthesised into a text that is coherent for the reader.

It is important that readers keep in mind the limitations of a study of this nature. A single case study 'is always only a composite picture of a limited part of the informants' reality, never the whole story' (Gudmundsdottir, 1996). That said, 'having partial, local, and historical knowledge is still knowing' (Richardson and St Pierre, 2005). As previously described, this research project used multiple methods of data generation as a way of increasing the credibility of the research. Denzin and Lincoln (2003) refer to the use of multiple data sources as triangulation, resulting in increased 'rigor, breadth, complexity, richness, and depth' (p. 8). Richardson (2003; Richardson and St Pierre, 2005) disputes the concept of triangulation, suggesting that traditional measures of triangulation used in the social sciences (see Denzin, 1978) are insufficient and that there are 'far more than "three sides" by which to approach the world. We do not triangulate; we crystallize' (p. 963). 'Crystals are prisms, which reflect the externalities and refract themselves ... What we see depends on our angle of vision' (Richardson and Lockridge, 2004).

With these thoughts in mind, the research design made efforts to crystallise the data (Richardson and St Pierre, 2005) through a number of ways. First, four school sites were studied, allowing for 'petite' generalisations (Stake, 1995) to be drawn by looking across the cases. Second, multiple methods of data generation (interview and observation) were used in each case site. Third, multiple participants (teacher, principal and several students) in each case meant that the data could be interrogated from several different perspectives. Fourth, a process of formal and informal member checking, repeatedly negotiating and revisiting the data with the participants, meant that the data presented in the narratives was less likely to contain misconceptions and misunderstandings (Ollerenshaw and Creswell, 2002).

Why Bourdieu and narrative?

Following the work of Barone (2000, 2001, 2009), the methodological framework of narrative inquiry was blended with Bourdieu's theories as a way of placing the narrative within a larger social context. Barone (2000) describes the critical theorist and the critical storyteller (or narrative inquirer) as 'authorial comrades-in-arms' (p. 193), sharing common ground and goals while pursuing them through different modes of discourse. Barone (2000) suggests that narrative (fictional and non-fictional) texts may provide opportunities for readers to engage in 'acts of conspiracy' (2000) and critical analysis (2001). Like Barone, Clandinin and Rosiek (2007) posit that 'narrative inquirers and Marxist-influenced scholars working in the applied social sciences often share an interest in analyzing the way large institutions dehumanize, anesthetize, and alienate the people living and working within them' (p. 47).

As a way of understanding the complex nature of the relationships between the teacher, their students and 'music', Bourdieu's concepts of *habitus*, *capital* and *field* were used. Bourdieu conceptualises *field* as a structured system of hierarchical positions that guide or regulate interactions within social spaces. Each field is regulated by a unique set of unstated rules. An agent's position within the field is determined by two significant factors. On one hand, the quantity and type of economic and symbolic resources – *capital* – they possess determines their starting position within the field, and their ability to compete for more capital, thereby further improving their position. On the other, the ease and instinctiveness with which they are able to follow the rules of the field depends on how closely the values of the field are mirrored in their own *habitus* – a socially acquired system of values, beliefs and dispositions. These three 'thinking tools' allow the interactions within music classrooms (as a particular type of social space) to be analysed in particular ways, explaining the processes by which the pedagogical actions inadvertently privilege some types of attitudes, preferences, knowledge and skills while marginalising others.

Bourdieu's work is congruent with the methodology of narrative inquiry in a number of ways, specifically in terms of epistemological stance and the role of reflexivity. Bourdieu's ideas on epistemology align closely with the constructivist stance associated with narrative inquiry, in which the role of the researcher is viewed as a crucial factor in the co-construction of knowledge. Bourdieu rejects the notion of an objective researcher (Bourdieu, 1999), demanding that researchers articulate their value stances, their problem choice and their theoretical and methodological frames.

> The positivist dream of an epistemological state of perfect innocence papers over the fact that the crucial difference is not between a science that effects a construction and one that does not, but between a science that does this without knowing it and one that, being aware of the work of construction, strives to discover and master as completely as possible the nature of its inevitable acts of construction and the equally inevitable effects those acts produce.
>
> (Bourdieu, 1999, p. 608)

In simpler terms, knowledge generated through social research can never be objective, rather, we must attend to the ways in which the researcher's presence contributes to and affects the construction of the knowledge.

Within this epistemological position, the reflexivity of the researcher becomes a crucial aspect of the research process. Drawing upon the work of Bourdieu, Rizvi and Lingard (2010) stress the significance of articulating researcher 'positionality', claiming: 'reflexivity demands transparent articulation of researcher positionality and the significance of this to data collection and analysis' (p. 48). Bourdieu takes this idea further, describing importance of 'reflex reflexivity', the researcher's ability to perceive, monitor and respond, in the moment, to the distortions brought about by the social relationship.

With these ideas in mind, in this research, Bourdieu's ideas are interwoven with the principles of narrative inquiry to create an approach to research that integrates theory, epistemology, method and methodology.

Reader's orientation

This book is structured in three parts. Part I provides a theoretical lens for understanding how the development of values and beliefs is interconnected with the social world. Bourdieu's concepts of habitus, field, capital, doxa, misrecognition and illusio are described, before discussing how they appear specifically in the context of the overlapping fields and subfields of music and music education. Using examples from contemporary literature around music education philosophy, theory and practice, I look particularly at the ways in which the habitus of music teachers and the doxa of Western music-making practices influence music pedagogy and curriculum. Notions of elitism, exclusivity, hierarchy and talent evident in Western art and popular music-making practices are discussed, including the ways these notions are reproduced or resisted in music education. The literature presented in this part contextualises the research questions and provides the basis for the critical reading of the case studies.

Part II presents the narrative accounts of the four cases. These chapters contain the stories shared with me by the teacher participants, and those of the schools' principal and their students, guided by my research questions. The narratives illuminate the ways that the teachers' values and beliefs shape their decisions about pedagogy, repertoire and curriculum, how they are enacted in the classroom and other settings within the school, and how they are shaped by broader societal and cultural forces.

Part III draws together the Bourdieuian framework and the literature described in Part I, along with the narratives, for the purposes of illuminating how the teachers' habitus and the doxa of music/music education are enacted in their classrooms, and how this impacts upon the music making and learning of their students. In particular, I explore the ways in which the teachers' musical values are communicated with students through the learning experiences, reproducing notions of a hierarchy of knowledges skills and musics, and, by association, a hierarchy of students.

Following writers such as Tom Barone (2001) and Christopher Small (1998), I have assumed that you, as a reader of this book, are 'perfectly capable of coming up with your own answers' (Small, 1998, p. 17), and have your own interest in and experience of music education. For such a research text to be critically useful, it should provide stimulus for a conversation between writer, characters and readers. As Barone suggests:

> The writer resists the compulsion toward propaganda, toward self-righteously tricking or bludgeoning the reader into accepting an agenda, however morally or politically enlightened. Writerly persuasion is of a different order, aiming to entice the reader into wondering about what has been previously taken for granted.
>
> (Barone, 2001, p. 179)

Each of the narratives presented in this book takes the form of a polyvocal conversation, with the voices of the teacher, principal, students and me being heard. At times some are stronger than others, sometimes they are heard solo, in duet or in counterpoint. At times they are dissonant, leaving unresolved tensions that require the reader to imagine the most satisfactory resolution. Further, my interpretations and analyses are merely one possible perspective – they are not exhaustive, and there are many other possible readings.

You, the reader, are tasked with the responsibility of interpreting the narratives in the context of what they might mean for yourself, in the context of your experience.

Notes

1 The term 'talent' is used here in a vernacular sense, to denote natural ability rather than Gagne's definitions of gifts (natural abilities) and talents (developed abilities or skills).
2 Details of the teachers and schools can be found in the introduction to Part II.

Interlude
Narrative beginnings

> As we tell our stories and listen to participants tell their stories in the inquiry, we, as inquirers, need to pay close attention to who we are in the inquiry and to understand that we, ourselves, are part of the storied landscapes we are studying.
>
> (Clandinin, 2010, p. 3)

With these words in mind, I begin with stories of my own experience of becoming and being a musician and music teacher. In the sections that follow, I explore my research questions, my values and beliefs about music and music education through vignettes of my own experience.

When I was teaching in school classrooms full time, the research questions described above weren't something I thought about at all: I didn't have time, there was just too much to do. This isn't to say that I didn't think about my teaching: I reflected on what and how I was teaching, on how I could get my students to participate more enthusiastically, on how I could make them see the importance of what I was trying to teach them. I had a clear idea about what I thought was important for the students to learn and how I thought they should learn it.

What I hadn't considered was why I thought it was important for them, or why it was important to me.

Becoming a 'reflective practitioner' was a large component of my education studies – I just didn't consider what I should be reflecting upon. My values and beliefs regarding what classroom music should be about remained tacit, enacted through my practice but untroubled by my reflective thought.

When I began my teacher education programme, I began to think about the way I had learned music at secondary school. While I had enjoyed and been successful in classroom music, I was dissatisfied with my experience as a model on which to base my own teaching practice. We listened to and analysed recordings of musics from a range of styles (but mainly Western classical music), we rehearsed for our performance tasks in small groups, we completed aural skills tests ad nauseam, and we completed compositions and arrangements, each painstakingly scored by hand. Some students in the class (me included) completed most of the work without too much difficulty, while others appeared to me to really not understand much of what was going on at all. I was particularly good at musical dictation. When we completed a dictation in class, our teacher would ask us to raise our hands to indicate how much we had completed correctly: all, most, half, or less than half. Across the two years of the Senior Music course, every time, it was the same students with their hands up for all or most correct, and it was those same students who also excelled in the other aspects of the course. Without exception, those students had learned instruments from an early age and participated in a variety of choirs and instrumental ensembles, at school and outside.

This wasn't what I wanted my classroom to be like. I wanted to be able to teach my students the skills they needed to do well, not rely on the students having developed them elsewhere.

I found what I was looking for in my teacher training programme. It was heavily focused on Kodály methodology – developing musical knowledge aurally and through use of the voice – and presented by a charismatic and convincing lecturer. I felt that I had discovered a way that I could make sophisticated musical knowledge and skills accessible to all my students, not just the ones who learned music outside the classroom. The clarity of the framework gave me a sense of empowerment; knowing that 'the method' had worked for other teachers, I was confident that I could make it work for me. Throughout my two-year teacher training course, I attended as much professional development as I could, gathering repertoire and strategies for use in the classroom, intent on mastering the methodology.

I began my first year of teaching confident in my own skills, but apprehensive about my ability to connect with the students. I was sure that I knew what was best for my students, that I could help every student to develop valuable musicianship skills (skills that I valued). I was convinced that I could win my students over and show them how much they could learn, if they did it my way.

My first lesson was with a Year 9 class, a class that other teachers had warned me were known to be difficult. My lesson was well prepared – we were going to start with a singing game to get them used to the idea that singing was just something we were going to do in music. I was nervous, because I could sense that these students were going to resist. Which, of course, they did. I persisted with the game for around 90 seconds before deciding that, in the interests of self-preservation, if I didn't try something different, I was in for a very difficult first semester of teaching with this class.

So I fell back on the only other experience of music teaching that I had to draw upon: what I had done in music at school. We talked and wrote about the history of rock music, I forced them to learn the basics of notation theory (because I knew it was good for them) and, if they got the written work done, the reward was prac – learning guitar, keyboard and drum kit. For the most part, the students were disengaged and uncooperative, and we rarely got to the prac component of the lesson. I blamed them for it, for not doing things my way from the start. My students were disempowered, and, I regret to say, really didn't enjoy music at all.

It was in 2005, while reading the work of Christopher Small (1998) for a Masters course in classroom pedagogy, that I first started to think about the culturally and socially constructed nature of music making. This was the first time I had questioned my own attitudes, values and beliefs about music making. Growing up as an apprentice within the Western art music tradition, becoming a good musician meant that you had to have a good teacher whom you saw for your weekly private lesson, you had to practise for hours every day, you had to do your theory homework. It had never occurred to me that there were other ways of learning and making music. As I read Musicking *(Small, 1998), I remember feeling shocked that I'd never thought about this before – about the elitist notions associated with music making in the Western art music tradition, about the rituals associated with concert going, about the hierarchy of composer, performer/s and listeners.*

I was a product and a reproducer of these attitudes. I would be the first to roll my eyes at the ignorant audience members who clap between movements of a symphony, at non-musicians' mispronunciations of the names of composers and works. At a concert of Mahler's Symphony No. 5, I remember applauding politely despite feeling a sense of frustration with the quality of the performance. The playing was lacking in energy, it was lazy: the brasses split notes in the fortissimo *sections, the strings weren't together, the conductor made grand gestures with no response in the orchestra's sound. The friend who I was sitting with, also a music student, turned to me while we clapped: 'Just hold up the score, and we'll clap for that', she said to me, as we, and the rest of the audience, continued our applause for an appropriate length of time.*

I was so attuned to the doxa of the social field that I didn't recognise just how elitist it was.

I was.

Over the next few years, as I read more and began to process these ideas about values and rituals of music making, I began to reflect upon the ways in which my own ideas about music making had been shaped by the values and beliefs of Western art music practice.

In turn, I began to consider the ways in which my values and beliefs had shaped the way I thought about classroom music teaching. I began to pay much more attention to who my students were and what they wanted and needed from music education. I began to see my role as a music teacher not solely as preparation for the very small number of students who would pursue a musical tertiary or career pathway, but as providing students with musical skills that would allow them to pursue music making of their own choosing.

Part I

Framing the narratives

2 Bourdieu's theory of practice

For the past century, the field of sociology of education has interrogated the structures, processes and power relationships that are so deeply embedded within the schooling system that they are frequently deemed to be 'normal' and necessary for learning to occur. The work of Pierre Bourdieu provides a way of analysing and interpreting these aspects of schooling systems, particularly the means by which pedagogical communication is culturally and linguistically encoded in ways that privilege students from dominant groups.

In this chapter, I describe a number of Bourdieu's concepts that are useful in understanding the ways in which music education is shaped by larger social forces, which are enacted through those with the authority to make decisions about music in schools. I begin by considering Bourdieu's concept of *habitus*, which explains how individuals become a product of their participation in various social spaces, before turning to his concepts of *capital* and *field*. These tools provide a means of understanding and interpreting the pedagogical acts that take place in music classrooms, looking at the ways teachers and students interact, the way music(s) mediate those interactions and the way they are shaped by traditions and histories of education and cultural production. Following this, I describe several other concepts that Bourdieu uses – *doxa* and *illusio* – that are useful for understanding the ways in which schools serve to reproduce dominant values and privilege.

Before continuing, a word of caution is appropriate. Bourdieu's concepts are complex and by no means incontestable (as is any interpretation of them). Bourdieu has revisited many of these concepts throughout his lifetime, creating layered definitions and meanings. His writing is opaque and idiosyncratic, and is frequently accused of being deliberately inaccessible.[1] The texts are not written pedagogically, and there is no reliable encyclopaedia of concepts. While Bourdieu encouraged scholars to 'put the theories to use' and rejected canonical readings of his work, there are contradictions in the ways it has been taken up, used and interpreted. There are a large number of misconceptions that have been cemented and perpetuated through publication, meaning that secondary sources (including this one) must be carefully evaluated in relation to the original texts. Synthesising Bourdieu's concepts that were used in this research into a single chapter, in a manner comprehensible to readers who may not be familiar with his work, has been a considerable challenge, and this has meant that there are inevitably places where nuance has been lost for the sake of brevity.

Relational sociology

> Social science has always stumbled on the problem of the individual and society ... The self-evidence of *biological individuation* prevents people from seeing that society exists in two inseparable forms: on the one hand, institutions that may take the form of physical things, monuments, books, instruments, etc., and, on the other, acquired dispositions, the durable ways of being or doing that are incorporated in bodies (and which I call *habitus*). The socialized body (what is called the individual or the person) is not opposed to society; it is one of its forms of existence.
>
> (Bourdieu, 1993b, p. 15)

Bourdieu (1989) describes his approach to sociology as 'structuralist-constructivism' (or equally, 'constructivist-structuralism'), looking simultaneously from both sides of the objective/subjective and structure/agency dichotomies. Wacquant (Bourdieu and Wacquant, 1992, pp. 7–11) describes this as necessitating a 'double-reading', to avoid deterministic reductions that view the social world as fixed and immovable, while at the same time explaining the resilience of social structures and patterns (such as reproduction of class).

Habitus

Bourdieu (1977) describes the habitus as 'an acquired system of generative schemes objectively adjusted to the particular conditions in which it is constituted' (p. 95). In simpler terms, the habitus is a system of 'acquired, socially constituted dispositions' (Bourdieu, 1990, p. 13) that are learned through our upbringing and through our participation in the social world.

Bourdieu (1984) describes the habitus as a 'structured and structuring structure' (p. 170), suggesting that it is structured by past and present experiences, that it is structuring in the way that it shapes one's present and future actions and that it is a system that contains an internal logic (structure). This does not mean that the habitus is rigid or fixed: it shapes the social world while at the same time being shaped by it. Thus, dispositions that make up the habitus are not immutable – there is space for change and self-revision (Wacquant, 2014b) – but the capacity for rapid or substantial change is limited by the constraints of the social space.

Bourdieu describes the habitus as the embodiment of 'a feel for the game'. When the habitus is closely attuned to the field, the agent is able to carry out the infinite number of acts that the game requires, which are unpredictable but limited in range. In his recent work on habitus, Wacquant (2014a) proposes three components to habitus: cognitive, conative and affective. He proposes that a habitus well aligned to a particular social space or field comprises an understanding of the specific ways of classifying things, people and activities (cognitive), the kinaesthetic skills that are developed through working within the domain (conative), as well as the motivation or aspiration to invest in the game affective.

A productive habitus allows for generation and improvisation of actions in unknown contexts based on what is known. Consider the behaviours that schools expect of young children: raising their hand to speak, making eye contact with their teacher when being spoken to, valuing reading and caring for books, sitting still and being quiet at appropriate times, following instructions. It isn't difficult to see that the children more likely to succeed in school are those who come from homes where similar things are expected of them, homes where their parents are very much like their teacher. Their habitus is far more likely to be attuned to the values of the field. Despite their age and role (young, student) affecting position within the field (making them low status), their habitus is attuned to those with high status (teachers, administrators), making it more likely that they will be able to improve their position in comparison with their peers.

As Maton (2008) identifies, Bourdieu's concept of habitus is enigmatic, easily and frequently misunderstood and misused. Wacquant (2014a, 2014b, 2015) cautions against 'theological interpretations that rigidly lock habitus into Bourdieu's framework' (2014b, p. 118), describing habitus as a multi-scalar concept that allows it to be put to pragmatic use in sociological investigations. He describes habitus as 'a capsule for a dispositional theory of action stressing that the agent carries her history inside of her and actively shapes her world through socially constructed instruments of construction' (2014b, p. 124).

Field

As Wacquant (Bourdieu and Wacquant, 1992) identifies, the notion of field and its specific use in Bourdieu's work is obscured by its seemingly obvious meaning. Bourdieu defines *field* as 'a network, or a configuration, of objective relations between positions' (Bourdieu in Bourdieu and Wacquant, 1992, p. 97). More recently, Wacquant (2014b) describes field as 'the invisible web of positions occupied by agents competing for ... authority and value' (p. 125).

A field is a particular type of social space that is characterised by autonomy – the degree to which it functions by its own set of regularities. As Bourdieu explains, 'in order for a field to function, there have to be stakes and people prepared to play the game, endowed with the *habitus* that implies knowledge and recognition of the immanent laws of the field, the stakes, and so on' (1993b, p. 72).[2] For example, the field of cultural production influences beliefs held about the inherently greater value of classical music compared with more popular forms. These judgements cannot be explained in relation to the sound properties of the music. An understanding of the field and its values provides a means of explaining the positions that various musics occupy.

Bourdieu frequently uses sport or 'game' as a metaphor for field, although he cautions that 'a field is not the product of a deliberate act of creation, and it follows rules or better, regularities, that are not explicit and codified' (Bourdieu and Wacquant, 1992). This is not to suggest that the interactions that take place within a field are objective or predetermined, but that the positions agents occupy within a field, and the relationships between agents, are predictable. The novice 'player' of the game must learn the rules and develop the skills necessary to play (a form of capital), if she is to improve her position within the field. Importantly, the rules don't feel like rules; they feel like natural, logical, autonomous actions.

Capital

Bourdieu (1986) uses the concept of capital to explain the resources and assets that agents make use of to improve their position within social spaces. While economic capital is widely understood, Bourdieu suggests that it is 'impossible to account for the structure and functioning of the social world unless one reintroduces capital in all its forms' (p. 83). In addition to *economic capital*, he proposes that *social capital*, consisting of social obligations and connections, and *cultural capital*, the cultural goods, educational qualifications and 'long-lasting dispositions of the mind and body' (p. 84), are resources that help to explain the unequal distribution of power.

Moore (2008) provides the example of the way the value assigned to an artwork is viewed as intrinsic (coming from the art work itself), when in fact it is arbitrarily assigned. The claim made by those who have the ability to appreciate or produce such works of art is that their involvement is disinterested, that they receive no benefit aside from personal pleasure. Bourdieu contends that these transactions are self-interested, that they are misrecognised exchanges of transubstantiated economic capital that serve to advance the agent's position within the social field. Professing to admire the particular type of music that is valued within a particular field, for example, gains status or capital that can be used to better an agent's position within the field. Think of a first-year piano student at a conservatoire, moving from a small town to the city to study. While this student could be expected to be intimately familiar with the works that she has studied, a broad knowledge of the entire piano repertoire – quickly identifying a piece by title and composer after hearing a short section, being able to discuss the composers whose works she likes to listen to and play – is capital that can be exchanged for power, being used to improve her standing in the eyes of her peers and teachers. The absence of such knowledge is a disadvantage, which may leave her relegated to the periphery of the field.

Cultural capital, which is most relevant to the issues in discussion in this book, can exist in three forms (Bourdieu, 1986): *embodied* (skills, knowledge and behaviours that are culturally valued), *objectified* (the possession of culturally valued goods: paintings, instruments, books, etc.) and *institutionalised* (by means of educational qualifications). Of these, embodied cultural capital is the most problematic, as it is most effectively transmitted through primary socialisation, from caregiver to offspring. Outside of primary socialisation, embodied capital is difficult to acquire, and therefore reproduces and strengthens existing class distinctions.

Moore (2008) draws attention to two purposes that Bourdieu's concept of cultural capital serves. First, that the values and tastes of social groups serve to stratify them, with some groups being elevated above others for reasons that are purely arbitrary and linked to power and symbolic violence. Second, that the same process occurs within fields, making distinctions between members of the same group or field. Membership of a social group does not imply a 'well-formed habitus', only that the habitus was 'well enough formed' to satisfy the criteria for entry. Capital is a way of explaining intra-group variance, and for essentialist and reductionist interpretations of class stratification to be avoided (Moore, 2008, pp. 102–3).

Doxa

In addition to these three main 'thinking tools', the concept of *doxa* is highly pertinent to any discussion of beliefs and values within a field of practice. If the habitus allows an agent to carry out the acts required by the game, the reason that they choose to carry out these acts (and not others) is because of their commitment to the doxa of the field. In essence, doxa are the silent and unspoken 'rules of the game', often misrecognised as 'the natural order'. 'Doxa is the relationship of immediate adherence that is established in practice between a *habitus* and the field to which it is attuned, the pre-verbal taken-for-granted of the world that flows from practical sense' (Bourdieu, 1990, p. 68, italics in original).

This 'practical sense' (or 'practical faith') is what allows those with a habitus that is closely aligned with the doxa of a field to succeed within the field where others may not.

> Practical faith is the condition of entry that every field tacitly imposes, not only by sanctioning and debarring those who would destroy the game, but by so arranging things, in practice, that the operations of selecting and shaping new entrants (rites of passage, examinations, etc.) are such as to obtain from them the undisputed, pre-reflexive, naïve, native compliance with the fundamental presuppositions of the field which is the very definition of doxa.
>
> (Bourdieu, 1990, p. 68)

Doxa is able to be maintained through what Bourdieu (2005) describes as *illusio*: a spontaneous and unthinking commitment to the logic, values and beliefs of a field. As Heidegren and Lundberg (2010) illustrate: 'Whatever the combatants on the ground may battle over, no one questions whether the battles in question are meaningful. The considerable investments in the game guarantee its continued existence. *Illusio* is thus never questioned' (p. 12). One example of illusio may be seen in the seemingly illogical sacrifices that many young classical musicians (and, indeed, their families) make for the sake of pursuing excellence in musical performance. The many hours spent practising, usually alone, and significant amounts of money invested in lessons and instruments, invested in a future career that doesn't guarantee a living wage, requires a strong illusio to maintain to the internal logic of the field.

Conclusion

This chapter has described and illustrated Bourdieu's reflexive sociology as a means of interpreting the social world. By conceptualising social fields as a spaces governed by a set of regularities with their own sense of logic, which value particular types of knowledge, skills and resources over others, we can see the ways that these systems both shape and are shaped by the values, beliefs, attitudes and dispositions of those within the field. This framework will be used to guide the discussion in the next two chapters, which consider in turn the field of music education and the forces by which it is influenced, and role of these fields in the formation of music teachers' habitus. It will then be used as an interpretive lens to illuminate the ways that the teachers' habitus shape their decisions, behaviours and actions in the classroom and other settings within the school, and how it is shaped by fields of music and education.

Notes

1 Transcriptions of spoken texts are perhaps the most accessible starting points (Bourdieu, 1993b, 1998; and especially Bourdieu and Wacquant, 1992).
2 Bourdieu suggests (Bourdieu and Wacquant, 1992, pp. 100–1) suggests that particular institutions or organisations can be shown to exert field-like effects but many do not. A detailed statistical analysis is required to determine whether the positions within an individual institution (university, school, etc.) differ from the larger field in a way that suggests it functions autonomously.

3   The field of music education

School music education, since its emergence in the middle of the nineteenth century, has been shaped by particular values and norms regarding what and whom music/education is for. As described in the introduction of this book, the purpose of this research is to interrogate the notion that music education is informed by the values of Western art music, resulting in exclusionary classroom practices. This chapter begins by describing the values of Western music making – following Bourdieu, termed doxa – that are arguably built around talent as a prerequisite for music making, stratifying people into a hierarchy of participation. This is followed by an exploration of the doxic effect that these ideas have on music education and the ways in which contemporary innovations have sought to work against these ideas.

On embarking on a discussion of the field of music education and the way it is influenced by fields such as Western art music, it is timely to consider Bourdieu's ideas that specifically relate to fields of cultural or artistic production, which he posits adhere to a unique set of regularities (1993a). Bourdieu argues that the field of cultural production is composed of two opposing subfields: the *field of restricted production*, where the goods are produced for an audience of those who produce of similar goods; and the *field of large-scale production*, which produces goods designed for non-producers. These two subfields adhere to different principles of hierarchisation, with the restricted production or elite subfield prioritising symbolic capital over economic, and the large-scale or mass-market subfield, like the majority of other fields, the inverse. These opposing subfields are a feature of all artistic fields, and, in terms of music, provide a useful way of understanding the way various types of capital are valued in different fields. 'Art for art's sake' is the mantra of the classical music world. Artists who cross over into more popular endeavours often lose some of their status as an artist, if the members of the eliet subfield get any sense that their success comes at the expense of their artistic integrity. Adopting the values of the mass-market subfield (economic capital) risks capital of the elite subfield, unless the product is also of high artistic value, as measured by the elite subfield. Despite the fact that the elite field generates less economic capital, it retains it's high-value status through arbitrary means (such as doxa and illusio. described in the previous chapter). It must, of course, be noted that in the case of music, the elite subfield is not entirely autonomous, as the production-only-for-producers principle does not hold across the entire subfield.[1] Production within the subfield could be conceptualised as positioned on a spectrum, more or less motivated by the value of symbolic or economic capital.

Doxa of Western music making: hierarchy, reductionism and talent

> If it is art it is not for all, and if it is for all, it is not art.
>
> (Schoenberg)

This frequently quoted statement by Schoenberg typifies an elitist view held by many within the world of Western art music: that it is not suitable for mass consumption. Within this view, the right to actively participate in music is reserved for those perceived to possess the necessary talent. This notion of talent being a prerequisite for music making is a widely held belief in Western cultures (Koza, 2001), although ethnomusicologists have long noted the stark contrast between Western music-making practices and those of some non-Western cultures (Chanan, 1994; Merriam, 1964, 1967; Messenger, 1958; Nettl, 1989; Small, 1998). There is an emerging school of thought within music education that identifies these attitudes of talent and elitism as not serving music education (Bernard, 2004; Bowman, 2007a, 2007b; Bradley, 2006, 2007; Regelski, 1998; Schmidt, 2005; Väkevä, 2006; Väkevä and Westerlund, 2007; Vaugeois, 2007; Westerlund, 2006), as they exclude some students from participating and devalue their previous musical experiences. The perceived superiority of Western art music is evident in some music education programmes, not only through the study of the canon, but also through the replication of its music-making practices in the general music classroom.

The role music plays in societies can be thought of as belonging to two broad categories: presentational music and participatory music (Turino, 2008). Viewing music for the purposes of presentation establishes particular understandings about music performance and musical roles. Presentational music carries with it the inherent association with notions of talent – that musical performing is something that some people do and some do not. Nettl (2007) suggests that presentational music is 'a metaphor for individual competitiveness, in which one admires particularly the performer's ability to do something difficult' (p. 832).

The tendency of Western art music (and, to a lesser extent, other Western musical styles) towards presentational music making and the audience/performer divide has contributed to the view held by many within the general population that performing in music is only for talented professionals. Large numbers of adults label themselves as 'musical' or 'unmusical', as 'talented' or 'untalented', these beliefs often being based on their childhood experiences of music (Bailey and Davidson, 2002). Kingsbury (1988) provides a hypothetical example of the child in the third-grade choir who is asked to mouth the words instead of singing with the other children. This child was most likely not told how to improve his/her singing, their only understanding being that it was singing that should not be heard. Further, the credibility of the teacher in making these judgements is not questioned, although his/her role in this scenario is of great importance. Such experiences are likely to influence a person's self-perception as 'unmusical', a perception that will most likely be carried into adulthood. When viewed in this way, it becomes clear that what it means to be labelled as 'talented' is subjective.

> The belief that musical talent is innate … divides children into the 'haves' and 'have nots', effectively prohibiting the 'have nots' from ever becoming 'haves' … Today, most music educators advocate music for every child, regardless of perceived ability, but few have considered the possibility that musical talent may be a social and cultural construct.
>
> (Koza, 2001, p. 249)

As Koza (2001) identifies, the belief in 'musicality' is so ingrained in Western culture that it remains largely unquestioned. This idea would seem quite curious in some non-Western cultures, where communities engage in far more inclusive musical practices. Merriam (1967) cites an American Indian tribe where all that was viewed necessary to be a good singer was 'good lungs' and a 'strong throat'. Likewise, Messenger (1958), while studying the Anang Ibibio people of Nigeria, found that everyone participated in the musical life, with children as young as five knowing hundreds of songs and many complex dances. He attempted to inquire about tone-deafness and non-musical people, but the people in this community found this idea incomprehensible. Merriam (1964) discusses the notion of specialisation and professionalism in music, stating that while there are some communities where specialisation or professionalism (e.g. being one of the king's drummers) is present, everyone is still able to make music well. Similarly, Chanan (1994) cites how the 'tribal community encourages and sustains a degree of musical ability in virtually all its members through widespread use of informal music' (p. 24). Within these cultures it is, of course, accepted that some people will sing or dance better than others, but that is certainly no reason for the less able not to participate alongside the most able (Merriam, 1964; Messenger, 1958).

Ethnomusicological studies into Western music making have drawn contrasts between these non-Western practices (Kingsbury, 1988; Nettl, 1989; 2007; Small, 1998). Within the Western art music tradition, there exists a hierarchical structure, a privileging of some musical activities over others and, by association, those who partake in them. Different roles of participation (performing, composing, listening) are assigned to different members of the community and members may only engage in activities that are considered appropriate for their level of skill and training. Composers are afforded the most prized place, for without them the Western canon of musical works would not exist. Anthropologist Lévi-Strauss (in Chanan, 1994) attributes the position of power that the composer holds to the way that they are the 'senders' of musical information, while other participants only receive. Given that a very small percentage of participants actually partake in composing, an unequal distribution of power is created. He compares this imbalance with the example of spoken language, in which all who receive are also capable of sending. Nettl (1989) provides an in-depth analysis of the idolisation of the composer, exemplified by the practice of carving images of such composers into the stone of concert halls. Small (1998) describes modern symphonic performances as 'summoning up the dead composer', a process he likens to a priest (the conductor) interpreting the sacred text (the score or musical work/object) of the prophet (the composer) and imposing his interpretation with those who come to listen (p. 89). As Nettl (1989) and Small (1998) identify, the highest status is reserved for a very select group of composers, most of whom lived 100–250 years ago.

Nettl (1989) and Small (1998) both view the practice of making Western art music to be highly hierarchical. Below the composers come the performers (largely so that the composers will have their works heard), with the conductor holding the highest position within these ranks. Bouij (2004) draws attention to the high status held by performers in the conservatory setting, and the view that non-performance endeavours (particularly music education and music therapy) are 'fall-back' career options. In the Western art music tradition, the performance of a work will never exceed the greatness of the work itself. A successful performance is credited to the composer, while an unsuccessful one will always be considered the fault of the performer/s, either through poor execution or poor choice of repertoire (Small, 1998).

The audience members, the listeners, are valued least of all, despite the fact that their financial support is the reason that the activity continues to exist. Their financial contribution aside, their presence is largely arbitrary. In fact, the idea of music 'for art's sake' places no importance on whether listeners appreciate or enjoy what they listen to, as it is not intended for mass consumption. This is exemplified in comments by prominent twentieth-century composers, Debussy being quoted as saying 'art is of absolutely no use to the masses', with Schoenberg presenting a similar opinion 'if it is art it is not for all, and if it is for all, it is not art' (cited in Scott, 1990).

In the symphony concert tradition, an invisible barrier exists between the performers and the audience. The performers almost never speak to the audience or communicate with them in any way except through the music of the programmed works (Small, 1998). The concert proceeds as if the audience were invisible, with only the conductor and concertmaster even acknowledging the audience's applause. If these behaviours were exhibited in a popular music concert, they would not be well received, the performers most likely being labelled as arrogant and 'out of touch' with the audience. These behaviours demonstrate the power relationships that have developed between the performers and audience through the 'sacralisation' of art music during the late nineteenth and early twentieth centuries (Levine, 1988). Levine describes performances during the nineteenth century, where it had been common for audiences to arrive late, leave early, talk, whistle or sing, shout requests for popular songs to the performers, eat, drink and smoke during performances (p. 182), practices that would be considered inconceivable today. Through a series of forceful displays by conductors and performers (insisting that the doors be locked during performances, stopping mid-phrase and waiting for noise from the audience to desist), this behaviour was eliminated from audiences by the middle of the twentieth century. For the remainder of the twentieth century, with the gradual removal of such informal social behaviours, Western art music has been viewed as the realm of the elite, not intended for the masses. There are an isolated number of cases where these practices are being challenged, with traditional art music and popular music contexts being fused in various ways. However, the traditional ritual of the symphony concert remains largely unchanged.

When considering the ways in which the doxa of the Western art music tradition are embodied in music education, it becomes evident that some of these values do not encourage inclusivity. Suggestions that school music is elitist and exclusive have been superficially addressed by the inclusion of non-Western and popular musics within many curricula. In light of the previous discussion, it would be apparent that the mere inclusion of repertoire from outside the Western canon would not fully address these issues, and that the structures and processes within traditional models of music education also need to be examined.

The discussion thus far has largely focused on exclusionary values in Western art music, although many of the same exclusionary structures can be seen in Western popular music. The notion of talent is again evident, with a large percentage of the Western population participating in music only through listening. These notions are particularly exemplified within the 'Idol' phenomenon (Fairchild, 2007; Stahl, 2004), where 'talent' takes on an elusive, almost mystical, quality in the ever-continuing search. Green (2001) draws attention to the impact of capitalism and consumerism on popular music practices, particularly ways that the music industry and media 'dictate norms of performance and composition that result from such high levels of capital investment as to be virtually impossible for amateur musicians to attain' (p. 3).

Doxa of music education

The doxa described in the previous section have informed and underpinned the philosophy and practice of music education in important ways. Historical accounts of music education philosophy identify two major philosophical movements during the last 50 years – Music Education as Aesthetic Education (MEAE) and what is known as the praxial philosophy (Alperson, 1991; McCarthy and Goble, 2002). The discussion that follows presents a brief overview of these philosophies and a review of how these ideas have been taken up and critiqued within the literature.

Music education as aesthetic education

Music Education as Aesthetic Education (MEAE) first emerged as a philosophy of music education in the 1960s. At this time, the major proponent of the movement, Bennet Reimer (1970, 1989c, 2003a), stressed the need for a unifying philosophy for music education, in order for the profession to gain credibility within the educational system. His work draws on the ideas presented by Meyer (1956) and Langer (1953) on emotion and feeling in music. Central to this philosophy is the notion of aesthetic experience, achieved through a distanced contemplation of works of art. Reimer (2003a) divides musical activities into 'aesthetic' – including listening, responding and critiquing – and 'artistic' – singing, playing, composing and improvising. He suggests that while a comprehensive general music programme should include a range of musical experiences, most of the general population choose only to participate in music through listening, and that the purpose of music education should be to meet the needs of these people by teaching them how to listen effectively (Reimer, 1989a).

Reimer (1989a, 1989b, 1997, 2003b) and others (Alperson, 1991; Woodford, 2005) have claimed that MEAE's focus on listening is motivated by democratic values, that all students are able to achieve success in listening activities. Reimer attributes the fact that the majority of the population engage in music only through listening to cultural changes, such as the invention of recording technologies and the availability of professional live performance. Others (Elliott, 1995; Koza, 2001; Small, 1998) would argue that many people do not perform because they are convinced that they do not possess the talent necessary to do so, that they exclude themselves from opportunities to perform on the basis of this belief. MEAE's focus on listening confirms the Western view that talent is required to participate fully in performing music and that the requisite skills to do so cannot be learned by all students.

Reimer (1997) suggests that programmes that focus on performing are elitist, in that they serve the needs of only a small percentage of the population – those who choose to actually perform (Reimer, 1997).[2] Woodford (2005) agrees with this, claiming that a curriculum based on performing inducts students into a narrow, hierarchical, elitist community, where 'non-musicians' or those of less talent are excluded or forced to become passive observers (pp. 32, 34). In effect, what occurs is that by removing performing from within the classroom, the only students who will ever experience music through performing are those whose parents can afford to provide them with lessons and an instrument.

MEAE has been criticised for the narrow view of music on which it is based, through the repertoire used, and the conceptualisation of music as musical works that is purely Western (Alperson, 1991; Bowman, 1991, 1993;

Elliott, 1995). As aesthetics has its roots in eighteenth-century Western philosophy, it is reasonable to suggest that it is a lens that is most suitable for the study of the music of that tradition. In the 2003 edition of his philosophy of music education, Reimer has attempted to demonstrate how the aesthetic lens can be applied to world musics, but, as will be discussed in the following section, this demonstrates a West-centric worldview and does not recognise the potential for other conceptualisations of what music is and the role it plays in people's lives.

Praxial music education

Elliott's praxial philosophy (1995) emerged as a reaction against MEAE's emphasis on listening and the aesthetic experience. Drawing on the work of Small (1977, 1987), Elliott takes the position that music is an action rather than an object, and that musical understanding is developed through praxis. Like Small (1998), he makes use of the verb 'musicing' to describe this action. He challenges the Western construction of composer, performer and audience (and, thus, the construction composing, performing and listening as discrete musical actions), embracing a multifaceted conceptualisation of musicianship that views these activities as interdependent.

Elliott (1995) bases his philosophy of music education on the idea that musical knowledge is essentially procedural knowledge, a matter of 'knowing-*how*' rather than 'knowing-*that*' (p. 53). This procedural knowledge can be acquired only through active experience of 'musicing' – the doing and making of music. He suggests that music is a complex phenomenon that cannot be completely reduced to verbal abstractions. Verbal knowledge about music (formal knowledge/'knowing-*that*') supports procedural knowledge, but, in isolation, does not constitute musical knowledge. First, music is an aural, temporal experience. This requires musicians to think in action, as music itself can be experienced only temporally.

Elliott (1995) is highly critical of the aesthetic approach, although he presents a singularly narrow conception of what the aesthetic entails. He suggests that the aesthetic concept rests on four basic assumptions: that music is a collection of objects or works, that musical works exist to be listened to aesthetically, that musical works have only intrinsic value and that listeners who listen aesthetically will achieve aesthetic experience (p. 23). Swanwick (1999) identifies this view as a caricature of Reimer's ideas (p. 6), suggesting that Elliott has provided an extreme account of aesthetic formalism. Swanwick, while supportive of MEAE in a number of ways, suggests that the 'aesthetic experience' is only one way of experiencing music, a position supported by Reimer in the most recent edition (2003a) of his philosophy.

While Elliott does not address democracy or inclusivity specifically in *Music Matters* (1995), there are a number of points in his philosophy that represent a departure from West-centric musical paradigms. In particular, Elliott disputes the idea of talent being a prerequisite for musical performance. Drawing on the work of Gardner (1983), he suggests that music is a form of knowledge rather than an innate talent, which, like all forms of knowledge, can be developed by all people in differing degrees of competency. 'Excluding the presence of congenital deficiencies, every person has the conscious powers necessary to make music and to listen for music competently, if not proficiently. Hence, all children deserve the opportunity to develop musicianship for their own self-growth, self-knowledge, and enjoyment' (Elliott, 1995, p. 235).

In other ways, Elliott's philosophy serves to preserve traditional power structures present in educational systems. Elliott states (1995, p. 259) that the aims of education are the student's self-growth and self-knowledge, with the intention of developing self-esteem and self-identity. Despite this, within this philosophy, the teacher is positioned as possessor of knowledge, being solely responsible for the development of the curriculum and learning experiences. Students are viewed as 'apprentice musical practitioners' (p. 266), being inducted, through the expert guidance of the teacher, into existing musical practices. Westerlund (2006) suggests that teachers are positioned as 'fully authorised carriers of knowledge' (p. 121), with students not expected to take a significant role in the construction of knowledge until they have increased their level of competence. This has the potential to function as what Freire (1972) calls the banking concept of education, whereby the students are viewed as deficient in the musical knowledge and skills that the teacher is able to provide them with.

A dialectical approach to music education

In an attempt to problematise the position of 'status quo' of music education that the previously described philosophies occupy, Jørgensen (2003) critiques these traditions of music education in the context of the highly fluid musical and educational landscape of the twenty-first century. While Jørgensen (2003) recognises the importance of traditions of music education, identifying the way they provide stability, clarity and continuity for the profession, she also draws attention to the ways in which they may function as an oppressive force, for those within and those outside of the system (p. 40–1). She rejects the notion that philosophies and traditions of music education need be seen as mutually exclusive dichotomies, advocating a more dialectical approach in which music teachers combine elements of different approaches, balancing these by choosing to focus more on one aspect before shifting focus to another as called for by the time and place. She encourages teachers to:

> break out of the little boxes of restrictive thought and practice and reach across the real and imagined borders of narrow and rigid concepts, classifications, theories and paradigms to embrace a broad and inclusive view of diverse music educational perspectives and practices.
>
> (p. 119)

Musical futures

One of the most pervasive global innovations in music education (except, perhaps, in North America) is the Musical Futures programme, developed from the work of Lucy Green (2002, 2008). Musical Futures makes use of informal music learning and popular music pedagogy, where students learn to sing or play music of their own choosing using the practices Green identifies as authentic to real-world popular musicians, primarily learning by copying recordings. The programme is designed to displace classical music as the primary material of school music, broaden the ways in which music may be learned in schools, deepen the level of engagement from students by connecting with their out-of-school musical experiences and to increase the number of students that see school music as being 'for them'.

A number of scholars have identified weaknesses in Green's work: oversights regarding the many ways that popular musics are learned other than by copying by ear (Clements, 2012), the danger of narrowing musical possibilities for students by conflating informal learning with (Anglo-American guitar-based) popular music (Allsup and Olson, 2012) and the potential for a focus on replicating 'real' musical practices to ignore the potential for music classrooms to create new musical realities (Väkevä, 2012).

Conclusion

This chapter has demonstrated the ways in which the values, norms and practices of Western art music have a powerful influence on music education. Notions of talent as necessary for music making and the hierarchy of musical participation have had a significant influence on what the purpose of music education is considered to be, and for whom it is intended. These ideas can be seen in the major music education philosophical movements of the late twentieth century, and, while there are pockets of resistance and growing trends towards displacing these ideas, they remain pervasive on the largest scale.

Notes

1 It could perhaps be claimed that genres such as contemporary concert music might be considered almost entirely autonomous, whereby only other musicians are interested in listening to it.
2 It should be noted that Reimer provides an expansion of musical roles in the 2003 revision of this text.

4 The habitus of a music teacher

It is widely acknowledged that teachers' values and beliefs shape their practice in powerful ways (Cochran-Smith, 1991; Fenstermacher, 1978; Pajares, 1992; Richardson, 1996, 2003). As described in Chapter 2, a person's habitus – the system of values, beliefs, attitudes and dispositions that guide our actions – allows agents to make spontaneous decisions in familiar contexts (fields), such as the classrooms in which they work. An individual's habitus is formed through their family upbringing and participation in particular fields. In this chapter, I describe in general terms the characteristics that are typically associated with school music teachers, drawing attention to the ways in which these attributes are shaped by experiences of learning in a Western art music context.

This chapter will explore the values, attitudes and dispositions of teachers broadly, and music teachers specifically, as described in the literature. Further, it will explore how these values are developed through their musical and educational experiences. The chapter concludes with a review of selected case studies of music teachers that demonstrate how the effects of the socialisation process are lived out in classrooms.

Socialisation of music teachers

It is well documented within the literature that many music teachers hold values that are inherited from the tradition of Western art music (Bouij, 2004; Bowman, 2007; Hargreaves *et al.*, 2007; Regelski, 1997; Ross, 1995). Hargreaves *et al.* (2007) found that teacher candidates with a background in Western art music may have little knowledge of other styles, and that this is inappropriate for classroom music teaching. They also suggest that their identity 'inevitably determine(s) how they project their own implicit views of the nature of music in the school' (p. 667).

As Richardson (1996) identifies, formal knowledge about any subject area impacts on the beliefs teachers hold about teaching and learning. While personal beliefs and values may be strongly held by individuals, such beliefs and values may not serve the interests of the students. Thus, educators have a responsibility to examine their own values and beliefs, and to question how these values impact on their students' learning. Like other 'specialist teachers', music teachers have most often engaged with the formal knowledge of their subject area for a number of years prior to or concurrently with their teacher training programme, and thus hold strong beliefs about what is valuable knowledge and skills in their subject area. Regelski (2012) suggests that music teachers in particular ascribe to a disposition he terms 'musicianism': teaching music in ways that prioritise musical choices and values over the interests and needs of the students and society (p. 21).

Richardson (1996) suggests that teacher beliefs are drawn from three main sources: personal experience, experience with schooling and instruction (experiences of teaching developed while a student) and experience with formal knowledge, both within their subject area and pedagogical knowledge. Richardson also suggests that the second of these – experience with schooling and instruction – has the biggest impact on initial preservice teacher beliefs, and that these beliefs often do not change during the course of the teacher education programme. Specifically considering music teachers, Regelski (1997) suggests that this propensity for teachers to model their school programme on their own musical training is particularly problematic, as it advantages those with a high aptitude for music and ignores the needs of the rest. He urges, 'the training of all students as though they might someday be conservatory students needs to give way to meeting the need for all students to be educated for a life-long amateur involvement in music' (p. 103).

This research concerning the ways in which teachers' values and beliefs resist change can be linked to Bourdieu's work on habitus. The durability of the values and beliefs related to what should be learned and how mean that teachers' practices are much more likely to be informed by their own experiences than through teacher education. Fenstermacher (1978) suggests that one of the goals of teacher education is the transformation of tacit or unexamined beliefs into objectively reasonable or evidentiary beliefs. Richardson (2003) cites a number of studies that have gathered empirical data on the success of changing the beliefs of teacher candidates, with the findings varying from little or no change to reported high levels of change. Tillema and Knoll (1997) found that while some student teachers changed their behaviour, their beliefs remained intact. Cochran-Smith (1991) suggests that beliefs changes that occur in response to academic courses are likely to be superficial, and that student teaching experiences negate these changes, resulting in the teacher candidate reverting to their pre-existing beliefs (Mills, 2012).

This work highlights the importance of understanding the ways in which teachers' values and beliefs, developed through primary socialisation and their experiences of education as a student, have such a strong influence on the type of teachers they become.

Music teachers' professional knowledge

There is a close relationship between personal experiences and professional knowledge (Jorquera Jaramillo, 2008). As Mateiro and Westvall (2013) claim, music teachers' knowledge 'is influenced by the cultural contexts from which it springs and the social contexts in which it is displayed, internalised and enacted' (p. 157). As described in the preceding chapter, historical traditions of music education have emphasised the importance of the 'canon', talent and teacher control (Benedict, 2009; Gould, 2012; Koza, 2001), and these have a significant influence on music teachers' dispositions, values and beliefs. Philpott (2010) suggests that music teachers' conservatism has contributed to a lack of innovation in music pedagogy. He states that, 'music teachers who emerge from school music, a university music degree and teacher education are highly likely to have been socialized into understandings which are informed by the western classical aesthetic' (p. 89). Where music teacher candidates are introduced to different ways of learning, such as informal pedagogy approaches like Musical Futures (Green, 2008), these approaches are 'bolted on' to their professional knowledge rather than being part of their own authentic experience of music learning.

Bradley (2012) points out that philosophies of music education as described above have the potential to act as a colonising force, closing down dialogue and advancing traditional ideologies of knowledge production (p. 411). When viewed as fixed, philosophies, theories, approaches and methodologies may perpetuate particular ideas through their un-thoughtful adoption and application in the classroom. As Gates (2010) suggests, historical traditions of music education practice are useful for providing grounding for novice teachers; however, if they do not respond to the ever-changing classroom environment, they create friction in the interactions between teacher and student. Bowman (2010) agrees, identifying the importance of reflective and responsive practice in ensuring that music teachers are conscious of the ends and purposes of their teaching practice. Juntenen and Westerlund (2011) support these claims, stating that there is value in the *grand narratives* or metanarratives of music education, where they are accompanied by the crucial element of reflection.

Case studies from the literature: values and beliefs enacted in practice

There is ample evidence in the literature that discusses the 'problem with school music'. In many cases, like the vignette from Ross (1995) that follows, the music teacher is blamed for these problems. The purpose of this section is not to continue this practice of blaming teachers, but to shine a light on the way that teachers' agency is limited by their habitus, how their experiences and dispositions shape what they see (and don't see) in their classrooms.

The following section provides a number of examples of existing knowledge of music teachers' values, beliefs and practices, demonstrating how they are shaped by the teacher's habitus. Some of these depictions align with the stereotypical representations of grand narratives of music teachers, while others are more nuanced, drawn from case study research. These examples from the literature illustrate the values and beliefs that music teachers hold, and how these values and beliefs are enacted in their classroom practice.

> The music teacher is typically a martinet, short on temper and quick on the pre-emptive strike. With an infallible and exquisite ear she banishes the growler to eternal damnation, getting shot of the unwashed masses as quickly as possible in order to bask in the rarefied company of the gifted exceptions. At seasonal intervals she is given a high profile and unqualified support as the school marshals its artistic forces for a public relations assault upon the punters; but for the most part she is quietly ignored as an eccentric and somewhat expensive queen bee.
>
> (Ross, 1995, p. 185)

Ross's depiction of the music teacher has been debated and rebutted at length (see Gammon, 1996; Plummeridge, 1997) and has been dismissed by some as nothing more than a caricature. However, there is a substantial body of literature, largely arising from the United Kingdom in the 1990s and 2000s, that describes a 'problem' with school music (Bray, 2000; Gammon, 1996; Mills, 1996; Plummeridge, 1997; Ross, 1995).

Drawing on her experience as an inspector in schools in the United Kingdom, Mills (1996) presents five extreme examples of approaching music education in the secondary school (in this case, for 11-year-olds). First, an approach that Mills calls 'sheep and goats', whereby the 'singers' are selected via audition to be part of the choir while the 'non-singers' are supervised doing not much at all. Second, a teacher who asks the students to tell what they did in primary school, while assuming that they have done nothing. In the third example, the teacher underestimates the capabilities of 11-year-old students. This is followed by the story of a teacher who praises the students regardless of whether their performance is worthy of praise, thereby denying them the opportunity to improve their work based on accurate evaluation. Finally, an approach that Mills describes as 'no keyboards before Christmas', where students are kept busy with writing activities designed to control and manage, and 'specialist resources of the school are withheld until the pupils have become so bored they are no longer likely to appreciate them' (p. 11). Mills admits that these examples are extreme, but that there are elements seen to a lesser degree in many secondary schools. While Mills's examples cannot be viewed as representative of all music teachers, they demonstrate evidence of some trends that suggest that some music teachers inadvertently or purposefully reproduce ideas that music making requires innate talent; and is thus for some rather than for all students.

Ballantyne and Mills (2008) analyse a series of interviews of a number of beginning music teachers using Gale and Densmore's (2000) framework for understanding social justice. They cite this example:

You get the upper level kids to play a melody, you can get the lower level kids to play just the bass part, just to keep the beat, and it keeps them involved and they feel like they're accomplishing something as well.

(Jess, 2nd interview) (Ballantyne and Mills, 2008, p. 82)

As Ballantyne and Mills identify, this example demonstrates a retributive view: a perspective of social justice that emphasises fairness in the competition for goods, suggesting that those who contribute more to society are entitled to receive differential rewards. To use Bourdieu's terms, there is an assumption that all students possess equal capital and a denial of the fact that they already occupy differential positions within the field. The teacher in this interview believes that the lower-level students will never be capable of achieving what the upper-level students can, and the pedagogical processes she employs means that they never will. This teacher places value on the extra-curricular experiences of upper level students (i.e. instrumental instruction external to that offered in the classroom music), which advantage their capacity to participate in the activities.

Rusinek (2008) provides an example involving a group of students in compulsory music studies who have been labelled 'disaffected learners'. Their poor behaviour in other subjects is starkly contrasted with their high level of engagement and self-regulation of behaviour in music lessons. Rusinek describes the way the teacher in this study has based his practice on Elliott's praxial philosophy (1995) by engaging students in performance activities in a class ensemble using Orff instruments and other percussion. The students had some choice over which part they played and which of the pieces would be performed in the concert; the teacher made suggestions about what he thought would be a good choice, but ultimately it was left with the students as a group to decide. All of these students learned all of the skills that they required within the classroom programme; there was no expectation of prior knowledge of music. This was only possible through carefully sequenced learning in rhythmic and melodic sight-reading, a skill that would allow them to perform more complex music than if they only learned aurally. Rusinek draws attention to this teacher's solution of 'complexity in response to diversity' (p. 19), by creating 12-part polyphonic arrangements, each part being of a different level of difficulty, with each student learning to perform several of them. While the teacher referred to this model of music education as 'working like the Berlin Philharmonic', from a social justice perspective, there were clearly different practices in action. The Berlin Philharmonic, like all internationally reputable professional orchestras, represents the epitome of elitist practices. The rigorous process of auditioning and trialling performers allows the orchestra to attain the highest possible standards of performance. Of course, within the professional music world, this is appropriate, given that the goal is performance at the most elite level. In Rusinek's example, there were no auditions; no student was deemed incapable of participating. Rather, the teacher and students held an expectation that all students could perform successfully, displaying a departure from the traditional 'talent' paradigm.

Wright's (2008) case study of 'Mrs Metronome' describes an experienced teacher trained in the Western classical tradition whose practice embraced popular musics and whole-class music making. Despite her attempts to provide an experience for her students that reflected their own musical likes and preferences, more than half of the students in Mrs Metronome's Year 9 class saw themselves as 'not real musicians' and considered the music that they played not to be 'real music'. The appropriation of popular musical genres into a formal learning environment reduced the 'real-ness' of the experience. Students reported desiring greater autonomy in choosing the music that they learned and the ways that they make and learn it.

The stories described by Wright (2008) and Rusinek (2008) have much in common: both teachers reject the notion of the 'unmusical' student, and provide ways and means for students to develop the necessary technical skills to participate in music making in the classroom. Students respond well to this approach and participate fully. However, hierarchical structures of control remain in place, preserving the dominant values about how music should be made and learned. The structure of the field (if we consider the individual classroom to be a field) has been opened up to allow all students to enter, but once they have entered, they have little or no agency or autonomy.

Tucker (1996) presents a case study of Joe, a classically trained music teacher in Jamaica. Tucker observed that Joe's pre-tertiary and tertiary music experiences reinforced his belief that music education is about achieving a high level of skill in instrumental or vocal performance. Further, it becomes apparent that Joe believes his students to be incapable of this, not possessing the necessary 'talent' to perform music well. Tucker notes how the students spend as little time as possible during the lesson actually making music, Joe preferring to keep them busy with menial tasks such as cleaning their recorders and thereby avoiding having to listen to the poor-quality music making that the students were capable of. If we compare Joe with the teacher in Rusinek's example, there is a stark contrast in the way the two teachers approached their teaching, demonstrating different values and beliefs about music education. Both of the teachers had been trained in Western art music performance and possessed a high level of musical skills. While Rusinek does not probe the teacher's beliefs about the students' capabilities, it is clear from the examples provided that the teacher believed the students to be capable of musical success. The learning activities were structured in a way that promoted successful performances from the students. In Tucker's case study, it becomes clear that Joe believed that his students were incapable of being taught, that they did not possess the necessary talent to perform music well. More than any other contributing factor, it was his beliefs about music and his attitude towards music education that stood in the way of his students becoming musicians.

Conclusion

The case studies described in this chapter serve to foreground the types of values and beliefs expected to be found in the fieldwork for this research. In particular, they illustrate the ways in which learning experiences are shaped by the teachers' habitus, at times resulting in practices that contradict what the teachers say they value. This highlights the usefulness of Bourdieu's theories as an analytical lens, allowing case studies to be interrogated and critiqued for particular purposes.

Part II

The narratives

This part of the book contains the narrative accounts that were developed with the participants in the field. The process of conducting the fieldwork was collaborative and recursive, with a high level of engagement from the participants ensuring that the narrative accounts are authentic representations.

Research context

In this study, schools sites were selected to represent a variety of contexts – co-educational and single-sex; state, independent and Catholic schools. The purpose of this was to investigate the degree to which sex, religious affiliation and socio-economic demographic influenced the approach taken by teachers and the impact that this had on their values and beliefs about music and music education in the lives of their students.

While schools were selected to represent a variety of educational settings, they all have established music programmes that are highly regarded within the community. None of the teachers are considered beginning teachers and most of the teachers have been teaching in their school for a number of years. This is not to suggest that the music programmes are of a comparable standard, simply that they have established programmes in classroom music (including Queensland Studies Authority Senior Music, The State of Queensland, 2004) and a performance music programme that has a presence within the school and in the wider community. The school sites in which the research was undertaken represent a range of approaches to music education and some diversity among the teachers' values and beliefs, although the student demographics were somewhat limited to largely middle- and upper-middle-class schools. Demographic details of the teachers and the schools can be seen in Table 1.

In Queensland, the school year is broken into four terms, each usually of between 9 and 11 weeks duration. This study focused on secondary schools, which in Queensland typically includes Years 8 to 12. Two of the schools (St Mark's College and Chiswick College) include some or all of the primary school years as well.

During the course of this research, several major reform agendas were announced. First, the inclusion of Year 7 in secondary schooling from 2014;

Table 1 Teacher and school demographic information[a]

Teacher	Age at time of study	Number of years teaching: total / at this school	Principal instrument	Workload	School	Private/public/ religious affiliation	Year levels	Student enrolments	ICSEA rating[b]
Michael Cook	44	25/20	Saxophone	Head of Music, Year 8, Year 11, Year 12, Year 12 Extension, Orchestra, Big Band	St Mark's College	Private, Catholic, all boys	5–12	1,482	1,116
Sam Hall	24	3.5/3.5	Piano/Voice	Year 8, Year 10, Year 12, Year 8–9 choir, private piano tuition	Chiswick College	Private, Christian, all girls	Pre-prep–12	943	1,086
Jan Laws	53	29/17	Piano	Year 8, Year 9, Year 10, Year 12, Year 10 English, Year 8 girls' choir, Year 9–12 girls' choir, Year 9–12 mixed choir	Blackfield State High School	Public, co-educational	8–12	1,506	1,080
Jayden Wood	31	10/10	Piano/Flute	Year 8, Year 9, Year 10, Year 11, Year 12, Year 12 Extension.	Seaview State High School	Public, co-educational	8–12	1,334	1,033

a All names of people and schools are pseudonyms.
b Index of Community Socio-Educational Advantage. A score of 1,000 is the benchmark, with higher or lower values representing degrees of advantage or disadvantage. Details on how this score is calculated can be found at http://www.acara.edu.au/verve/_resources/About_ICSEA_2014.pdf.

and second, the release of the draft shape paper for the Australian Curriculum. Staff members in some of the schools discussed the future impacts of these reforms; however, due to the fieldwork spanning a period of almost two years, they appear more prevalently in some cases.

All four schools had an instrumental and choral music programme that operated in parallel with the classroom music programme. In each case, these programmes were long established and well utilised, with between 10 and 30 per cent of the school's students taking part.

Relational responsibility

The narratives draw upon elements of critical theory as a way of situating the experiences of these individuals within the broader social context, the research remains faithful to the ontological and epistemological commitments of narrative inquiry. Clandinin and Murphy (2009) write, 'as we compose research texts, we are attentive to the practical and social justifications of our work and to how we can best respond to the necessary research questions "So what?" and "Who cares?" But as we do this, we cannot sacrifice our ethical commitments to our research participants' (p. 600).

Clandinin and Connolly (2000) describe a sense of 'relational responsibility' (p. 177) that narrative inquirers must have for their participants. This responsibility shaped every aspect of this study, from the initial negotiations of access to the school sites, to the final stages of manuscript preparation. At times, there were tensions and contradictions within the data that could not be explored without sacrificing this responsibility and jeopardising the research relationship between the participant and myself. This resulted in differing levels of analysis and critique between the narratives, depending on the nature of my relationship with the individual participants. I describe below how my relationship with each of the teacher participants shaped the data and the final research texts.

Michael: Michael appeared to approach the research, and my presence within his classroom, with an attitude of mild ambivalence. He answered my questions, freely offered information about the music programme and the school, but he wasn't highly engaged in the research process. If my interpretation differed from Michael's, he dismissed mine as the misinterpretation of an outsider, but was comfortable for multiple perspectives to be included in the final texts.

Sam: Sam and I communicated comfortably from the beginning of the research process, having met several times before and sharing many common acquaintances. We also shared similar backgrounds in teacher education, having attended the same institution (although at different times). While Sam initially came across as not particularly interested in the research but happy to let me do what I needed to do, he treated my interview questions thoughtfully and spent many hours reading and commenting on the interim research texts.

Jan: For me, this research relationship was the most difficult to negotiate. More than the other participants, I felt that Jan positioned me as an expert who was in her classroom to judge her teaching practice. She often gave me unprompted explanations for what she was doing in a particular lesson, as if she felt the need to defend her practice. She asked for my opinion on a variety of topics, requesting repertoire ideas, how to approach the curriculum reform in which the school was currently engaged. I struggled with how to respond to these requests, not wanting to appear unsupportive but reluctant to cast myself in the role of expert or consultant. Part-way through the observation period, Jan asked me to stop coming to her choir rehearsals, as she felt that my presence was affecting her preparation. For the second formal interview, I constructed my questions with extreme care, feeling that the questions I wanted to ask would make Jan so uncomfortable that the interview would become tense and the research relationship irreparably damaged.

Jayden: My previous relationship with Jayden is described in the prologue to Chapter 7. In many ways, Jayden was the opposite to Jan: confident that her view was 'correct' and quite willing to point out where she thought I had misinterpreted the events. I found that my questions to her needed to be very direct, almost confrontational, as playing the 'devil's advocate' seemed to be the way to encourage Jayden to elaborate on and justify ideas that, to her, were 'common sense'.

Variations in implementation

In the two Education Queensland schools (Blackfield and Seaview), the research application needed to be approved by the Department of Education, Training and the Arts (DETA) Strategic Policy and Research Office. There was a wait of several months while the application was considered; hence the fieldwork commenced in the two private schools before a response was received. The initial research proposal submitted to DETA was rejected, as it "did not strongly align with the department's current priorities". It became apparent that removal of the term "social justice" from the research proposal would result in a more favourable outcome. The proposal was revised and approval was granted. The revisions required modifications to the interview schedule for teachers and principals. For example, principals at St Mark's and Chiswick were asked about their understanding of "social justice", while principals at Blackfield and Seaview were asked about "diversity".

Terms, definitions and acronyms

The following definitions are the way these terms are commonly used by music teachers in Queensland, Australia.

'Prac' (practical work): A term commonly used by classroom music teachers when referring to lesson time spent singing or playing instruments, individually or in groups. Prac lessons (or partial lessons) are distinct from 'theory' (any work that is purely written), 'aural' (work that involves listening and possibly writing) and 'composition' (students typically working on group or individual composition projects).

Class: A group of students, usually between 15 and 30.

Classroom music: An academic subject that involves a broad range of musical knowledge and skills, that may include singing, playing instruments (usually keyboard/guitar/recorder/Orff percussion instruments), listening to recorded music, analysis, composing, improvising and/or conducting. It is not anticipated that classroom music will take the place of tuition on an instrument/voice. In some parts of the world, classroom music is called 'general music'.

Lesson: Period of time that the teacher spends with a particular class on a particular day.

Performance music programme/instrumental programme/ensemble programme: In addition to the classroom music programme, each of the schools had an extra-curricular music programme that includes individual and/or small-group lessons and ensembles. Lessons may occur during class time (usually on a rotating timetable so the student doesn't miss the same subject each week) or outside of class time, depending on the student's/parent's/teacher's preference. Ensembles usually rehearse before school, after school and in lunch breaks rather than during the regular school day.

VET: Vocational education and training, usually taking the form of nationally recognised certificate courses that students undertake as part of their academic programme.

5 Michael Cook at St Mark's College

Located in a leafy, upper-middle-class suburb, not far from the city center, St Mark's College is known in Brisbane as a prestigious Catholic school for boys. The College has been established for over 50 years, with a powerful Old Boys' network, and some students attending the school are the third generation of their family to do so. With this in mind, as I enter the school, I am expecting to see images of a grand religious tradition. Instead, I am greeted with a view of impeccable, modern sporting facilities on both sides of the driveway. I soon discover that this is not the main driveway into the school at all, but the back entrance. After consulting my street directory I find my way around to the front of the school and am met with exactly what I was expecting: immaculate grounds, mature trees, leading to an impressive white building perched high on the hill. As I begin my trek up the hill on foot, I soon discover that the structure I had assumed to be the centre of the school is deserted.

A conveniently located map allows me to find the administration building, where I wait for my interview with Mr Ferguson, the Head of School. Gayle, Mr Ferguson's personal assistant, with whom I have been exchanging emails to set up this appointment, greets me warmly. While I wait, I have time to observe what is on display in the reception area, and I again encounter a strong sense of tradition. Eight large banners representing the College 'houses' (used for grouping the students for the purposes of sport and pastoral care) are prominently displayed. The portraits of the past Heads of School line the walls – all male, all Brothers, with the exception of the recently appointed Mr Ferguson, the school's first lay principal.

When Mr Ferguson is ready, I am shown down the hallway to his office, where I am greeted somewhat more reservedly. His office is a scholar's office – a large desk, dark timber bookcases lining the room, large windows looking out over the picturesque but student-free entrance to the school. I think back momentarily to other occasions I have been in principals' offices – as a student, as a prospective employee, as a teacher going to a meeting with 'the boss'. This office is more opulent than most. Mr Ferguson and I are seated on either side of a small coffee table, with my recording device between us. Our exchange begins hesitantly, and I wonder if my questions aren't specific enough, if he's not sure what I'm asking (or if I'm not sure what I'm asking!). Within a few minutes there seems to be a shift in momentum, and Mr Ferguson begins to elaborate on the ethos and philosophy of St Mark's College, with social justice featuring strongly within the values of the College. 'What I think social justice is I'd go to what it says in Matthew's Gospel ... Jesus' words were "do unto others as you would have them do unto you". In the twenty-first century I say to these boys here "treat other people how you would like to be treated". And I think that, you know if we could get that happening then there certainly wouldn't be any issues. You know, and it's not a perfect school and it's not a perfect world, so that doesn't happen, you know there are hiccups from time to time.'

At the time, I wonder about the 'hiccups' to which Mr Ferguson refers, although I get the impression that he doesn't wish to elaborate. A few days later, while walking past the assembly hall I notice security cameras in the area where the students keep their bags. These cameras come up in a conversation in the staffroom, where another teacher informs me 'bullying and theft are a huge problem here. You wouldn't think so in a school like this, but they are.'

A sense of 'do unto others' is perhaps more evident in students' interactions with people outside the college community. 'The boys are also very conscious here about ... not so much the rights ... within the college, but certainly the need to care for those less fortunate who live outside [in] the community. We have a fairly strong ministry programme here called MATES: MATES stands for (St) Mark's Are Taking Everybody Seriously. And boys get involved in the junior school and also in the high school in various opportunities to help those who are less fortunate than ourselves ... Every Wednesday night, one of the college minibuses attaches a trailer to the back of it and that trailer has a fold out sort of BBQ area and we go down to a park not far from the William Jolly Bridge in West End and provide ... food and drink for people who live on the street. [It provides the boys with] a real awakening of how some other people live. Some of the boys have really good interaction with the people that attend the BBQ and some of the boys obviously feel a little bit intimidated, so they hang back.'

'It's a bit confronting for them', I say.

'Oh, absolutely. But they certainly get a good opportunity to see how some people in our society live ... that's quite significant.

'We also run a camp here called the Sony Camp and it's largely for disabled children. [These children with physical disabilities] have an opportunity to come and live in the [College] community and boys become sort of like their minder or their buddy and they care for these kids for the week and have the opportunity to interact with them. I think they take them down the coast one day and they go to Dreamworld or Movieworld[1] or something like that. But they have the opportunity to help people with a physical disability. And Rachael, I can certainly say that, at the school I was principal at before here, there was a boy who has been to the Sony Camp and he came and spoke to me about how positive his experience was. It was one of the best things that he's done in his life so you know it gives a nice opportunity for kids with physical disabilities to interact with boys at the college here.

'The ministry section that's very strong in the college runs MATES that I just talked about, they also offer immersion programmes. And the immersion programmes give boys the opportunity to go and help overseas. Some examples of what happens in the immersion programme is that our boys have the opportunity to go to the Solomon Islands and visiting a school there and it's on an isolated island – it's not on the main island or anything like that. So they have the opportunity of providing assistance you know in a project on this particular island in the Solomons. Boys also have the opportunity of visiting a school in Alice Springs for indigenous children and have the opportunity of working with them. Boys have the opportunity of going to Phnom Penh in Cambodia where there's two Brothers that run a school that's totally for disabled children. So they go over there and basically teach some English to the children plus also participate, where possible, in some sort of activity where they build something you know that's needed over there. There's also a fourth one that's being offered to Year 11s this year is the opportunity to go to Vanuatu and participate in a small school community there as well.'

I ask about the boys that participate in those programmes. 'Are they in it for a holiday, do you think? I mean, going to Vanuatu for the school holidays sounds pretty exciting.'

'Umm ...' Mr Ferguson seems slightly taken aback by my question. 'Yeah, sure. I suppose you could look at it from that perspective and think that they're going to get something out of it as far as that's concerned like a trip overseas or something like that. Yeah, I would imagine that there could be an element [of that] before they go, but certainly when it was launched the other day with the Year 11s, a Year 12 boy spoke and he was one of the boys that went to Cambodia last December, and I don't think by the time he came back there was any idea that it was a cheap overseas trip.'

Music at St Mark's College

As I enter the impressive, new-looking music centre, my eyes first fall on the plasma screen TV, advertising upcoming events, communicating messages to the students about instrumental lessons and broadcasting video footage of leading international performers. The receptionist's shiny new iMac, the view of computer labs and recording studios up the hallway immediately draw attention to the importance placed on resources and facilities in this department.

Michael Cook, the teacher I have come to interview, is Head of Music at the College. His responsibilities in this role include supervising the three other classroom music teachers, conducting the orchestra and big band, and teaching Year 8, 11 and 12 music and Year 12 music extension. When I arrive, I am told that he has forgotten that he has yard duty at the time we had agreed to meet, so I am shown into the staffroom to wait for him. As I enter the staffroom, my arrival interrupts the teachers' discussion of the latest assault allegations against a prominent sporting star. The conversation ceases, introductions are made, and the inevitable conversations follow, trying to discover 'where do I know you from?'. Two of the instrumental teachers and I had done our undergraduate degrees together. This is then followed by enquiries as to what I am doing here. As I explain my project, several teachers seem eager to talk about it, while others drift away and continue their discussion about the footballer.

Introducing Michael Cook

When Michael arrives, he shows me into his office, where we will complete the interview: simple but modern furnishings, the desk holds an iMac and MacBook, the bookshelves are filled with CDs and music DVDs. His saxophone stands in the corner. The windows overlook the theatre on one side and the interior of the music centre on the other, allowing for cursory supervision of students from within.

I am caught a little off guard by the reception I receive from Michael – he seems to be a little blasé about participating in my study. He responded so promptly to the email received from me via the Head of School that I was expecting a more enthusiastic interest in my research. Upon reflection, I expect that I was confusing lack of interest with simply being busy and having a researcher distract him from his already heavy workload.

When I ask Michael what made him volunteer to participate in my study, he says that he really wants people to see what's going on in his school. 'I always say yes to prac teachers [because] my main thing is to make music for everybody and I just like people coming in and seeing different things … I think that the more people that can see things done in different ways the better. I just sort of feel like I'd like to see every school have, you know, three classes of Year 12 music and a third of the [cohort] doing music, and the more people see it and see it's realistic the more chances of it happening. That's basically it.'

Michael's pride in the programme that he has developed at St Mark's College is obvious. As head of the music department for the past 12 years, Michael is the person largely responsible for the size of the programme and the development of the facilities. In his mid-forties, a teacher of 25 years' experience, he professes a continuing enthusiasm for his work. 'I would consider that I would keep doing what I'm doing into my 60s and maybe even my 70s, because I don't really see it like I'm coming to work. I feel like I'm coming to do something that I love.'

Musical beginnings

'My Dad worked for a bank so I went to a lot of different schools … I went to a different high school every Year in 8, 9, 10, 11 and 12. At the school I went

to in Year 8, there was a Brother that offered an instrumental music programme and I got into it ... I found music was one thing that I could do well
... basically when I went from school to school, music was the main thing that
I had that held my ... education development together. It gave me a common
thread that I could take from school to school.

'My parents weren't into music. My mother [had been] made to do music
and hated it ... and my Dad came from western Queensland, Cloncurry ...
there was no music out there in the '40s and '50s, so [I had] no encouragement
from home ... I was given an instrument [by the school] to start off with, but
then I had to provide an instrument so I got a paper run and bought it. Mum
and Dad weren't that interested in it ... They weren't unsupportive, but it was
foreign to them, and they sort of thought "oh well, if you want to do it then
you can do it". They gave me a bit of money towards my first saxophone, but
basically I went out and worked and got one.'

As I reflect upon this, I am struck by the determination shown by Michael
in the absence of parental support. Many Queensland schools have an instrumental programme where the students are given an instrument for the first
year of lessons, as Michael was. Typically, the absence of financial support
and encouragement from parents would eventuate in lessons ceasing, no matter how powerful the support from the teacher or school. This experience
seems to be an example that resists Bourdieu's theory of capital. Bourdieu
describes music (along with other cultural pursuits) as being part a 'disinterested' transaction, as the investment in it produces no tangible economic
benefit, only symbolic cultural capital. Bourdieu (1986) suggests 'the initial
accumulation of cultural capital ... starts at the outset ... only for the offspring of families endowed with strong cultural capital' (p. 246), that it 'cannot be accumulated beyond the appropriating capacities of the individual
agent' (p. 245). Where and how did Michael accumulate this capital? What
motivated Michael to invest so much into something on which his family did
not place high value?

'Being a saxophone player, my main interest was really jazz ... I don't know
how that ended up being because my peers weren't that into jazz and my parents weren't into jazz but that's just what I was into.'

Michael describes the group of adult jazz musicians whom he learned from
by attending their jam sessions. 'When I moved to Cairns when I was about 14
there was a culture there, a jazz culture of a jam session ... And I would turn
up there, had only been playing the saxophone for a couple of years, and I'd
sit in with old guys, most of the people at these things were in the 40s and 50s.
But you know it was just the experience was getting up [and playing] – I could
play the tune and then the improvisation would start and I just realised I had
no idea what was going on. So I started trying to get hold of records, which
was hard in Cairns – most of the record shops didn't have any jazz ... I started
copying people's solos and transcribing them, playing by ear.'

My thoughts return to Bourdieu's theory of capital, this time in the way
that the social capital provided by this community of musicians allowed

Michael to develop his musical skills in ways that would not have been possible in his music making at school. It also gave legitimacy to his music making, something that he needed in order to continue.

'[When it came to career options, Mum and Dad] sort of questioned [the validity of music] ... when I was getting serious about it when I was moving into later high school, [they had concerns about] where music was going to be leading for a career. What my parents were trying to say [was] "well, where's the job going to be in?" I had to start thinking about if I'm going to go to the Con and do music where's it going to end up. The reality is a lot of people maybe especially entering performing courses probably think that they're going to be a performer. But I just knew that that wasn't really a possibility because, you know, I knew that [the saxophone] wasn't an instrument in the orchestra, that I couldn't get a full-time job. It is interesting though how it turned out because like out of all the people that did performance at the Con I actually did end up playing, not full-time with the orchestra but I ended up being a casual player with the orchestra. Yeah, so it was just like, I just realised when I was in high school that if I was going to pursue [music] as a career I had to look at career pathways and so I knew that teaching was where I was going to ... end up. Instrumental music teaching appealed to me a lot more than classroom music teaching did at the time. But that sort of has changed a bit, I suppose because I've ended up teaching just classroom music.'

Michael elaborates on his reasons for this change. 'I did it find it a bit tricky with instrumental teaching because, especially in a school like this where the kids have to pay additional fees for their music lessons ... so they have to have the correct amount of lessons in a term. So in a big school you have lots disruptions, with you know sport or events or whatever and trying to administrate and fit all the students in and teach classroom music at the same time, just wasn't really that feasible. So I ended up pretty much going over all to classroom teaching then since I've been here as head of music, which has been a fair while now, I've just taught classroom music.'

Michael's values and beliefs about music education

'My [ideas about being a musician] change all the time. It was actually quite interesting where we had a meeting at the end of last year between, with all these different musical organisations talking about the future of music education and the implications of the national curriculum ... There was a fairly senior academic in my discussion group and he made an interesting point, in the fact that musicians, it's only really in the last 100 years or so where a musician is a "teacher" or a "performer" or a "composer" or a "musicologist". Before that time [musicians] were performers, they were composers, they were musicologists, they were everything, they were all-rounders ... And that's sort of really where I see myself as a musician: I'm a person that still likes to perform, I still practise because I want to. [I started] thinking that, yeah, sometimes I see music educators that sort of cut off a part of their musical life, they cut off their performing, or whatever. Being a musician for me it's not really a job, it's a way of life, you know?'

As Michael continues describing what he values in music education a number of beliefs emerge: music being a subject for everybody, music being like a holiday, the power of teaching by deception, the need for music education to deal with 'real' music and the necessity for a music department to be well resourced.

Music for everybody

'Making [music] open to everybody and also being fairly open and diverse with the styles of music that we do ... I think the thing that we're trying to promote in the school is that music is for everybody. It's not just for the kids that [know they] want to do it – we're trying to find kids that don't realise they want to do it. So in Grade 5, 6, 7 and 8 we're trying to show them all these different things about music ... and probably half of our kids that do music as a subject might have always thought they were going to do music, but then on the other half were people that just weren't considering it at all. So it's trying to make it accessible to everybody and give them the opportunity to do well at a subject ... It's made really obvious [when kids elect to take classroom music] that it's for everybody, you know, it's not just for people that have learned an instrument before that already know how to play.

'Like I keep on saying, Year 8 music is what we call the "sales module". You know I'm not too worried about assessment – we definitely assess them – but I'm not giving them a test every three weeks or four weeks. I'm just getting them to have an understanding of what music is as a subject, it's performing, composing and listening to music and analysing it. And then in Year 9, when you have them the whole way through until Year 12 you've got a lot of time to teach them a lot of stuff. But if in Year 8 you try to teach them too much they don't do it in Year 9 and 10. I'm not saying you're not trying to teach them [too much], but trying to assess them too much ... I think it turns them off the idea of keeping going with music.'

This 'music is for everybody' approach has resulted in St Mark's College having a very large enrolment in Senior Music – consistently around a third of the cohort in recent years – with a number of students having no musical experience outside of the classroom programme. Alongside those students, of course, are students who have lessons in the school's instrumental music programme and some who also participate in elite youth orchestras.

'You know like we've got a kid here that's, you know, lead cello with the second orchestra for QYO (Queensland Youth Orchestra). There's no point in him coming in the class here and playing cello 'cause he can play it in the orchestra ... in classroom music we'll try to get him to play something different, like, you know, new skills, play the bass, play the guitar, play the drums ... Definitely when it comes down to an assessment item I'll advise the kids "okay, yeah, you know you're Eighth Grade in the trumpet you should play

... the Haydn Trumpet Concerto", and he'll get an A+ for it. But those kids can do that anyway because they're taking private lessons outside of school. They're not learning that here at school, they're learning that from the private teachers.'

This is reflective of the constant balancing act of a music teacher, trying to meet the musical needs of the whole spectrum of students with diverse musical backgrounds, including the high achievers and the less experienced. From my own experience in the classroom, I found it difficult to know where to begin, how much time I could spend on basic musical concepts that some students desperately needed to understand in order to pass the course, concepts with which other students were already very familiar.

'I always make the assumption that, I know it sounds strange, but the kids know pretty much nothing, you know? But I think, with the analysis work, trying to simplify things helps ... like, eventually you've got to use the jargon, but at first, talking about teaching things in levels, just trying first off to say okay this bit's repeating the same thing over and over again, can you hear what this instrument's doing and this instrument's doing and trying to get them to listen inside the music a bit more. I start talking in terms and I look around carefully at the kids if I started talking about sonata form or start talking about binary form or ternary form. I'll have a quick look around, and if I get the vibe through their body language that they're all with me I'll continue using that term. But I'll keep a close eye out for the kids that don't want to keep eye contact and look away and then you just know that they're not with you.'

'So those terms aren't something that would've been encountered in Year 8 or 9 or 10 music?', I ask. 'Some of them, no', Michael says. 'Some of them might have encountered it, but it's just gone in one ear and other. They haven't digested it, they haven't really grasped it ... I'm more into the "hands-on" stuff, and I think we've got other people on staff that we make sure in Grade 8, 9 and 10 they do understand theory and how to put a chord together and stuff like that.' As Head of Music, Michael has around half the usual teaching load – the 'other people on staff' to whom he refers are the three other classroom music teachers.

'Music like a holiday'

I ask Michael why he thinks the programme has such large enrolments and what attracts the students to take music in the post-compulsory years?

'Basically, I think also the kids see it as an alternative to some of their other subjects, that it's a bit of a change, like a holiday, coming down to music. We try to make it more hands-on, make it attractive. They see it more of as a subject where they're coming down and having a good time ... The general idea is that when the kids come into the music centre that it is a different place to any other part of the school. That the classrooms are set up differently, the kids are encouraged to come down at lunchtime and to have access to the equipment, and most lunchtimes there'd be 60 or 70 kids down here doing things [on the computers or in the studios].'

The classrooms do look different from regular classrooms. The walls are lined with benches that house the computers and keyboards. The centre of the room is an open space, where the students sit either on the floor or on chairs without desks.

This idea of music being a break from academic routine is evident in all of the lessons I observe. The students are given a lot of freedom to complete the work in their own time. This means that some students appear to waste a lot of time, drifting from one thing to another. Michael conveys to me that he is happy for the students to work in this way, that they need to discover things for themselves, including the need to take responsibility for their own learning. 'I find that the analysis assignment works as a bit of a wake-up call – some of the kids go "Oh my God, I'm going to have to, you know, pay more attention and ask more questions." And they'll tend to do better the second time around, and with this syllabus (The State of Queensland, 2004) that's fine because they only need one of the marks to count – the assignment at the start of the year or the analysis exam at the end. There's a real variety you know ... There are some who really push themselves and get stuck into it though, you know. One [essay] I've just read, I thought "I couldn't have written that": it was just such a high standard of work.

'The kids need time to explore, so here we give them time and space, we try not to overload them with too much assessment.' This sentiment is echoed by Charlie, one of the students I interviewed. He says, 'Some people I think take it [music] as a bit of a bludge. I mean the assessment isn't as rigid as say history and anything like that ... Music's not as, or can be not as, hard going as other subjects ... There's less assessment and we always get lots of class time to do it.'

Michael admits that some students do waste a lot of class time, but that they get the work done in the end. He prefers a less structured class environment 'because real life is unstructured. They have to learn how to do things for themselves.'

In some ways, Michael appears to be taking on some of the essentialised notions of boys' educational needs (Lingard *et al.*, 2009), such as preferences for kinaesthetic learning and using technology (Green, 1999). However, another recurrent theme within the literature is boys' apparent preference for structured programmes with explicit, direct instruction (House of Representatives Standing Committee on Education and Training, 2002). The relatively free approach that Michael adopts in his classroom would appear to go against this.

'I suppose [the approach I take is] based a lot on how I learned. Like I said, I went to lots of different high schools, and that was an interesting experience ... changing schools all the time, I would see lots of different teachers.

'Basically how I came to get [the skills I needed to work as a musician] was by working it out myself ... I just thought that the more structured way of learning – in a way it's a lot simpler. You've got everyone going down the same path; you've got defined parameters so you [as a teacher] really have to know less, because you can say, "you don't have to know that, it's not on the exam". For me, I saw that a lot of the things that I did exams on at the Conservatorium were irrelevant to what a real musician needed to know. I really am a big believer in "what you learn in life, you learn yourself", you know. So that's basically how it came about – we set up structures that gave the kids long-term projects to work on, with not so many boundaries.

'I never got these ideas through studying or a methodology – it just came through a culture of setting up that I thought would work for these kids. And it's changing all the time based on what results from what the kids are doing. What matters in the end is what the kids can produce.'

In other lessons, students are required to work within slightly more limited parameters because of the space that is available for their class to use (practice studios rather than the classroom with computers). On one particular occasion I observe students working in small groups (between three and six students) in practice studios that are equipped with electric guitars and bass guitars, as well as electronic drum sets. The students are in Year 11 and have a performance assessment coming up soon – they need to prepare one piece or song of their own choice (any style or genre, any combination of instruments or voices). I have chosen not to enter the studios to observe the students working – the rooms are quite cramped and my presence would undoubtedly alter the work patterns of the students. Instead, I remain outside the studio, out of the students' range of vision, but able to see and hear what they are doing through the window. Michael describes the group I am observing as being 'nearly ready, pretty together'. The students drift from one song to the next quite independently of each other, occasionally temporarily coinciding and playing together before going off on their own path again. The students are, at times, seemingly oblivious of the others in the room, while at other times showing off for their peers. These rehearsal practices reflect some aspects of Green's (2002) study of informal learning practices utilised by popular musicians and Abramo's (2009) study of the ways in which boys and girls work differently in musical groups. My initial thoughts about these students' working echo those of some of the teachers in Green's project – 'judging by what happened the week before, I didn't think they'd have anything ready' (Green, 2008, p. 37).

When I discuss my observations with Michael afterwards, he suggests a simpler explanation. 'If you went in there and said "play me the song", they'll do it. In a situation where they've got a deadline coming up, it's the kids who haven't been working all the way through the unit are generally panicking and playing their songs, the kids who've got it together are just sort of going through the motions. So they've got their work done, they had it together.' Anxious to show me that this is the case, Michael searches for the video recording of the students that I was observing on that day. He shows me performances of other groups in the same class, which are indeed of a very high standard. He says, 'I wish I could find those students, just to show you.' I assure him that I believe what he's telling me. (Michael emails me later with links to the videos.)

Michael continues. 'But also, it's [music's] not just about a holiday. Every year the school get's about ten OP 1s[2] – some years a few more, some years a few less. While there is usually about a third of the Year 12 cohort taking music, nearly always half the OP 1s do music. The evidence is there – more of the brightest kids in the school are taking music. The kids see it as worth their while. Also, we almost never have really talented performers who don't take classroom music – it must be giving them something as well.'

McEwan's (2006) case study, which was conducted in a school with a similar demographic to St Mark's, found that students who participated in instrumental or vocal ensembles and had lessons outside of school often choose not to study classroom music because of the presence of an alternative means of pursuing their musical interests. It must be recognised, however, that the number of variables in this type of comparison is immense: the content and approach of classroom music programmes, the number and desirability of alternative subject choices, the school culture and family values and circumstances have the potential to impact upon students' decisions to continue with elective music courses.

'Teaching through deception': learning without realising

Michael describes to me how his approach to teaching was shaped by an experience in Year 12 Biology: 'We just went to the mangroves for a whole term ... We did all these field studies ... and basically I thought we were just having mud fights' – I laugh – 'that's all I could see that was going on! And then when we got to the end of the unit we went back to the science lab and the teacher had all these stations set up and we had to name everything. And I went through it and I knew everything! And I thought, "Man, I didn't think I was learning anything. I thought I was just having a good time." Like, I thought I was actually being disruptive, I sort of was, but even though I was thinking about being a teacher I thought, "Man, that is a really cool way to teach." I call it "teaching through deception", you know, and that's the sort of a bit the way we started here, where it's hands-on, learning to play all these things because they [the students] want to do it.'

As I listen to Michael describe this experience of informal learning, I am reminded of his narration of the jazz jam sessions in which he participated at around the same time in his life. Clearly informal learning experiences have had a significant impact on Michael's own learning and on the way he teaches now.

Typically, informal learning relies on the students having a high level of intrinsic motivation and engagement, which is certainly evident in Michael's own experiences. However, I wonder whether Michael's students really are intrinsically motivated to learn, or if they're more motivated by the assessment tasks. I wonder whether some of the boys could learn more, whether there is a way of striking a balance between freedom and structure? I wonder whether the boys have the maturity to challenge themselves, to be autonomous, or whether Michael could play a larger role in guiding and scaffolding the learning experiences?

'Real music'

'I like a really hands-on approach to music. I think music should be about making real music. We really try to encourage them to explore different things … kids will bring in all different types of music and we'll listen to it and explore it and generally the way we have so many kids engaged in music is 'cause we sort of get into what they're into and try to learn about that … so it's trying to get the kids aware of different things.

'A lot of the times it's showing the kids different styles and then giving them time to explore that style or explore, you know, we'll show them how to do something on Sibelius or show them how to do something on Logic, which are different software packages … They can create, you know, they can do things … on a very creative level and make real music. Maybe on the other hand though, they mightn't really understand what chord they're creating or what notes are in the chord.'

I ask Michael about whether he thinks it's important that they understand what it is they're composing, or that they could write it out if they needed to.

'Well no, as far as writing it out, if they're not going to be communicating with other musicians that are notators I'm not that worried about it. I'm sort of hoping that they'll understand how to make real music. How to put a real composition together, how to make a CD or how to produce a score that's not in theory, that's actually the real thing.

'Music notation is just a form of recording … just a recording tool to be able to communicate music. And the kids can still do that through audio, you know, like now they can play, they can do a composition, they have to have understandings of harmony and structure and to do a good piece of work, but they can just record it, mix it, turn it into a real piece of music and they can send it, you know, across the world within seconds.

'I know any day of the week, any class I could go to, any class at this school, whether it be a music class or a maths class or any class and say "nobody's going out the door until you can tell me all the notes on a bass and a treble clef". I can teach them that in 10 minutes and they'll all get it. And maybe give me 20 minutes and I could teach them the basis of rhythm. And they could all do it. But once they walk out the door, unless they use it again they're going to forget it.

'[On the other hand] if they need to use it, I think it's important that they learn how to do it. As a professional musician, working as musician … I would go play with the orchestra I had to read fluently. You couldn't turn up there and say "can you play it to me?" Playing in a pit, like I played in shows

... you know, like you get two rehearsal calls and you're in doing the show ... to be totally honest even the trained musicians that I have worked with, the fluency that you really need to be a professional musician, not that many people really have it. Before I was a professional musician I could read music, but then when I got into that environment where they just chucked this whole book of music in front of you and some of it was quite tricky I just realised my reading skills aren't as ... you know, I can read music but really reading music with pages and pages of it without stopping and not making mistakes. [Being a fluent sight-reader is] a really highly developed skill. So here in the school I would say ... if the kids want to do that, really we couldn't teach it through classroom music. You know, I don't think you're going to be able to teach a student how to fluently sight-read music in classroom music where they're also having to do like analysis of music, composition, you know, their practical performances, I don't think that you're going to be able to teach that in high school, to fluently read music. But I would hope that they would go out, they would understand what treble and bass clef was and how rhythms work and all that sort of other stuff.

'When I look at the general musical community you really do have to be able to read music. Yeah, I think if you're a music teacher ... there's so many things going on with music, [reading] is one of the things that you definitely need to know how to do. But I don't think that if you're just wanting to do the subject music, like in a normal subject, I just can't see if I wanted to make them all fluent sight-readers of music I'd pretty much have to be doing that the whole time. And I just feel like it's a matter of priority ... of what skills we want to teach them.

'If the kids want to learn [to read music] it's a great thing to have. It's one of the skills that I enjoy having that I can pick a piece of music up and be able to play it ... But, I mean, there's a lot of music that you don't get out of a piece of paper that you get from listening to someone else or several different people playing it. And I just feel like that even the classical musician, like if I am playing ... a classical piece I feel like I have to know it by heart. You don't ever go to a concert and see ... well, you very rarely go and see a soloist playing concerto with the orchestra with music. Because what they're doing ... I mean, they definitely had to read the music to get it, but they tend to only really get into the music side of it once they actually know the thing off by heart ... they're not looking at dots there, they're hearing things in their head.

'When we went from the old syllabus (The State of Queensland, 1995) to this syllabus (The State of Queensland, 2004) where we went from kids having to do written scores [for compositions], and having to provide a score for any performance that they did, I was interested to see how [removing those requirements] would go. But here, from my experience here, the outcome has been a higher level of musical performance and composition. Through performance I've seen it in the fact that a lot of kids instead of having to worry about making sure they're following the piece of paper they're more worried about making an actual piece of music.'

State of the art

My first impressions of physical resources as a focus in the music department prove to be true. The amount and quality of the equipment is nothing less than phenomenal – two fully equipped music technology labs with 20 computers each dedicated entirely to music, four practice studios with electronic drum machines and a full complement of amplifiers, as well as more studios for the instrumental teachers that can be used for student practice.

'I think for me resources are a fairly big thing. It's not the be all and end all, but I just find that the kids think it's exciting when they come and there's something new, you know, "what have we got that's new, how does this happen, what can this do?" If you can, if you're up with [the technology] and you can show them how to do it, then they get excited about it and it becomes a lot more meaningful for them. I've spent a fair bit of time in the holidays like investigating resources, whether that be just music scores, recordings, equipment but I would spend, you know, couple of weeks in the Christmas holidays getting all the stuff happening.

'Initially we didn't have all these resources. I think that if you're doing music as a subject I think that you need to have some instruments and you need to have some tools for doing it. And I think back to the old days when there wasn't computers in the music classroom and there wasn't instruments for kids to access, the subject was more a mathematical sort of subject – you know, it was just the score and making sure all the harmony rules were followed. I think resources are really important and a lot of people too will come in here and look around and say "Oh, no wonder it's so good – you've got all this stuff."

'But I would say if I had to do it over again, I'd just go back to square one, and that was like get a couple of old computers from some other departments that didn't want to use them. That's how we started off. And music is a subject that you can use for fundraising, if you really have to, quite easily. Also, you can resource a department cheaply if you need to – like you can go down to the newsagent and buy a music magazine that has, you know, free software downloads, it doesn't cost you anything. If I had to start again, I'd probably bring some of my own stuff in too. I think to make it a successful subject you've got to have things, you got have instruments, you've got to have tools for the kids to be able to play with.

'I'd sort of hope that when they leave the music programme if they don't go on to tertiary music studies, which only between three to six kids do each year … But they could go out and play and compose … and now that computers are so accessible that they'll have access to that and they can do it. I think to be truthful a lot of things about, you know, "Bach was born in 1685 and died in 1750 and blah blah blah blah blah", I think that they might know that but for me a lot of times they'll just forget that. I would just rather them to be able to go out and be able to play and be able to compose. I would hope that music becomes a real thing it's not something that they learned about theoretically ... When they finish school that they enjoy it ... like if they enjoy sport, you know, like, they go out and they might continue to play club football. In music, they mightn't be in a community orchestra ... but they'll have a guitar or a piano or have a sing and be able to have those skills that are real skills that are accessible to them.'

'Even if it's just something for their own enjoyment', I add.

'Yeah.'

Music in context: the whole-school picture

The first day of my observations is assembly day. When I arrive at the music centre, Michael is already up at the hall setting up. Michael tells me, 'this doesn't happen every week, having the orchestra on assembly, only a couple of times a term'. I am warned that there won't be much teaching happening during the first double lesson – Year 12 music extension – as a large proportion of the class are in the orchestra and will be preparing for the performance.

The assembly begins with the usual 2 rituals. The traditional owners of the land are thanked, the national anthem is sung and the college prayer is recited.

An enthusiastic group of students, complete with costumes, make their way from the back of the auditorium while 'Eye of the Tiger' plays over the PA system. The purpose of this presentation is to encourage the student body to collect sponsors for and participate in the school walkathon. This is followed by another group of students reporting back on the recent rugby tour to Tonga. The photos projected of the students playing their matches and socialising with the local teams are greeted with enthusiasm by the student body.

The time has come for the orchestra to perform. The MC announces the name of the piece that will be performed and eyes turn towards the corner of the hall where the orchestra is seated. For the first time since the assembly began, there is a low murmur of chatter from amongst the students. Michael Cook, their conductor, raises his baton and then waits for the noise to subside. It does not. After a few seconds he lowers his arms. Other staff members then begin to shush the students, temporarily increasing the level of noise. I wait for the Head of School, or in fact anyone, to move to the microphone to reprimand the students for this disrespectful behaviour, but no one does. Michael then decides that he cannot wait any longer, raises his arms again, and the orchestra begin to play.

The piece selected for the assembly is the March from Bizet's *L'Arlésienne* suite. I notice a few of the students (mainly string players at the back of the section) clearly have very little idea of what's going on, trying very hard to look like they're playing along with the others. (I later discover that these are the same students who attend rehearsals rather infrequently.) This is the minority though; the group's performance on the whole is cohesive, with a few standout performers.

The piece finishes loudly, with brass and percussion blaring. Polite applause from the students and staff follow. And the assembly continues …

A staff member comes to the microphone to speak about the upcoming Middle School Arts Night. In contrast to the previous few items, the students are entirely unresponsive to the brief but unengaging invitation to attend the event.

When the Head of School makes his address, he thanks the staff and students of the big band who travelled to Goondiwindi (approximately four hours' drive west) for performances the previous weekend. I find it a little curious that there isn't a student report prepared for this, considering how well received the student presentations reporting on the sporting trips were.

In our conversations, Michael has told me that music and sport are equally valued at St Mark's College. However, based on my observations of the assemblies that I attended, there seems to be a disparity in the culture and attitude of the school between sport and music and the arts. At an institutional level, there is certainly evidence of increased financial investment into music, particularly in the last few years. Michael tells me, 'I have tried over the time and it sort of has been successful … that we're really well resourced here and, as I said, when I started 20 years ago the amount of money put into the music programme compared to the sport programme was vastly different, whereas now … it would be similar sort of monetary things going into music and sport, if not probably more into music.'

Certainly, significant gains have been made, from a school where 15 years ago, all of the students played rugby, and big band rehearsal had to be after rugby practice (5–6pm), to a school where there is a group rehearsing almost every day before and after school and approximately a third of the senior cohort take music as an elective subject. But, from my observations, I feel that there is still a sense that music is a less valued activity. I ponder the possible reasons for this: is it something about the types of musical activities that the students engage in that doesn't engender a whole-school culture of music making? Is it that the systemic patriarchy is so deeply embedded that music will always be considered a less 'masculine', and therefore less valued, activity? Is it that the school believes that an equal financial investment in music and sport reflects an equal sense of cultural value?

It is almost a year later when I discuss these wonderings with Michael. 'Isn't that funny, I don't even remember that performance. I appreciate that that's how you saw it, but I'd probably have to disagree. I can see where you're coming from, but I also think that it's partly because you're an outsider. The culture of an all-boys' school is really different – having 1,500 males with almost no females – it just doesn't happen very much in the broader society. If you're not part of that culture it's probably easy to misinterpret things … It's hard to get an accurate view when you're just coming in and coming out.'

I wonder about what he is saying here: is he positioning me as a (female) outsider, excusing my misinterpretation as a way of justifying his own interpretation? Or is he trying to justify the boys' behaviour?

'I asked some other people about this too, about whether they think the kids talk too much. And they were obviously murmuring, and that's why I stopped. I would say, generally, compared to the other schools that I've taught at, the assemblies are relatively quiet.'

'They are – I agree with you', I say. 'It was almost silent for the whole assembly. That was the only time that there was any talking from the students at all.'

Michael goes on to describe to me how the culture has changed in the time that he's been at the school. 'When we built the new music centre, about five years ago, we had the first concert ... it was a real eye-opener for me as a musician – I think sometimes we get caught up in our own worlds. When we had the concert, like, parents came in with pizzas; they came in with little kids and colouring books and like spread them out on the floor in the aisles of the theatre; they were bringing cans of drink into the theatre. Some parents were letting little kids run onto the stage while the kids were playing. I was just in shock, you know. As someone that takes their kids to concerts – not that often because it's expensive – but my kids, and I think other musicians' kids, would know that you don't walk onto the stage while the musicians are playing.'

The social rituals associated with concert-going that Small (1998) describes were clearly not part of the school's culture. 'In an area like this, you'd think that there'd be a fair percentage of the population that would have gone to some concerts and would understand these things. So basically at the next concert I had to get up at the beginning in the foyer and talk to all the parents and kind of give them a mini-lecture about "you know, it's great that we've got this new facility, we've spent a lot of money on it, we'd prefer you not to eat or drink"; and go through what you do at a concert, you know, "that the kids have put in a lot of time and effort into the performance today, they need to concentrate, we can't have people coming onto the stage". It took probably a year of me emphasising that before the parents all got it.

'The whole process was really mind-boggling for me, because I'd made all these assumptions on how I thought parents would react in this sort of situation. And I think it shows that music isn't really part of the culture of these families.' I'm reminded of Bennett, Emmison and Frow's (1999) study, which provides considerable evidence to support this. They suggest that differences in 'culturedness' – participation and consumption of cultural goods and products – between different economically differentiated groups are less pronounced in Australia than in European societies (pp. 264–5).

Michael continues, describing how he believes Australian gender stereotypes shape the boys' attitudes towards music. 'The kids don't – and I don't think this is just at this school, I think it's a much more broad Australian male cultural thing – they're just much happier saying "I like rugby". You know, they feel comfortable with it ... they're not taking a risk when they're saying that they're into sport. If they are more artistically inclined, they're less likely to come out and say that in a public forum. The kids are a lot more comfortable showing enthusiasm for sport.'

As I transcribe this, I pause to consider how much this says about the school culture. This is the first time in my visits to St Mark's, including my interviews with Michael and with Mr Ferguson, that masculinity has been raised as a topic for discussion. I wonder about the relationship between the broader culture of masculinity and cultures developed in all-boys' schools? Is there potential for resistance of hegemonic values?

Michael describes how there are different practices seen in the uptake of classroom music within the school. 'With music here, you can see how much it's changed over the last couple of years, and well, they're picking music as a subject. I feel that the kids are voting with their feet in choosing to do music. I think your observations [about the school culture] are accurate, but I think the nature of the school culture is changing, but how they are in the classroom is different to how they are in a public setting. And that comes from the broader male Australian culture more than anything from this school.'

As Michael said earlier, the choices he has made about the classroom programme at St Mark's, particularly the types of activities in which the boys take part, are chosen because they are attractive to the students. The use of technology, a focus on popular music instruments such as drums and guitar (Green, 1999), as well as an avoidance of singing and 'feminine' aspects of composition such as writing lyrics (Green, 1997; Harrison, 2009; Koza, 1993) allow boys to participate in classroom music activities without 'risking their masculinity' (Plummer, 1999).

Michael's comments also draw attention to another conflict, in the way classroom music and extra-curricular music activities are positioned within the school, with a significant disjuncture in the participation levels between these two programmes. St Marks' instrumental performance programme is more 'traditional' in nature than the classroom programme – concert bands, orchestras, string ensembles and choirs – and is thus a counter-stereotypical activity. The ensembles at St Mark's are of a reasonably high standard and size, which is not unlike other schools with a similar demographic. However, the number of students involved represents a significantly lower percentage of the school population than the classroom programme. Harrison (2001, 2003, 2008, 2009) suggests rigidity of gender stereotypes and Parker (1996; Plummer, 1999; Pollack, 1999) fear of homophobic abuse embedded within participation in the arts as possible reasons for some boys' reluctance to participate in performance ensembles.

The influence of hegemonic masculinity on school music making and wider participation in the arts has been discussed at length, in theoretical and empirical studies. While there is evidence to suggest that there is a cultural shift taking place at St Mark's College, significant aspects of stereotypical masculine remain unquestioned and unchallenged.

Leaving the field

As I leave St Mark's College, I reflect upon the inconsistencies in the data, on the tensions and contradictions within the story that are not easily resolved. St Mark's has developed a classroom music programme with one of the highest levels of student participation in the state. Michael has worked hard to make music an appealing option for the boys, a subject that is seen as different from other academic areas.

Michael's teaching is heavily influenced by his experience as a student, incorporating aspects of teaching that he enjoyed and learned from, and reacting against ways of teaching that he disliked. Michael's teaching is characterised by freedom: the boys are given time and space to explore musical styles that they like through the classroom programme. His 'hands-on' classroom environment seems to appeal to them, although there were times when I got the impression that they were waiting to be given a new song to learn or a new task to complete.

Michael's desire to make music 'a break from routine' in some ways has been accomplished: music at St Mark's looks remarkably different from a typical secondary school classroom. Michael prefers a practical approach to music learning, and this is delivered at the expense of theoretical understanding. Choosing to focus on the practical, students in Michael's classroom spend the bulk of their class time playing instruments and composing using computer software. Is the absence of a contextualised study of notation a way of allowing greater access to learning or is it limiting access to a deeper understanding of some musics to those students who learn outside the classroom programme?

This leads me to ponder the purpose of a teacher. In his classroom, Michael takes the role of a technical assistant, a project supervisor or resource manager. And there are a lot of resources to manage – computers, a wide range of instruments, microphones and PA systems, practice spaces, a recording studio. What the students do with those resources is left largely up to them; the students are expected to provide their own direction and motivation. I wonder whether some of the students would learn more with some more structure, whether they 'cruise' until the assessment task is due because that's all that's being asked of them. Or are they learning more because of the time that they're given and the freedom to explore?

Stereotypes surrounding boys participating in music would suggest that it is more difficult to make music attractive in an all-boys' school setting. Michael has fought against a 'rugby culture' for many years, working to create a musical culture in which the boys will willingly participate. In many ways, he has achieved this, with very high numbers of students participating in elective courses, with high levels of success. In other ways, the attitudes associated with hegemonic male discourses prevail at St Mark's College. There is almost no singing in Michael's lessons. Social value assigned to instrumental ensembles appears to align with Adler and Harrison's (2004) hierarchy, with jazz and concert bands considered more acceptable than orchestras and choirs. I know of other all-boys' schools that experience similar difficulties, and I find myself wondering whether this is just the nature of music in boys' schooling or if there are ways of building a school culture that rejects hegemonic stereotypes of masculinity that position the arts as feminine.

Notes

1 Local theme parks.
2 OP: Overall Position, the ranking system for tertiary entrance in Queensland. OP 1 is the highest ranking.

6   Sam Hall at Chiswick College[1]

I arrive at Chiswick College feeling notably more confident than in my previous research site – mainly because I know where I'm going, having visited the junior school several times in the previous year to teach an enrichment programme. Like many long-established schools, the College is a school that has far outgrown its original buildings, with new classrooms added in a rather haphazard manner. With several street entrances, a lack of maps and signage, Chiswick is not an easy site for visitors to navigate. Even though I am familiar with the school, I can't find the Senior School office where I need to go to sign in, so I decide to go directly to the music staffroom, in the hope of receiving further directions from there.

When I arrive at the music staffroom, I am greeted by Sam Hall, the teacher I am here to observe, who is busily planning this morning's lessons while the other teachers are at a staff briefing. The rabbit warren-like staffroom is a maze of hallways, with far too many desks for the space available. As the other teachers (and several preservice teachers) return from their meeting, the space becomes crowded. There are more people than chairs, so visitors stand in corners, trying to leave room for others to move through the cramped space. As the morning bell approaches, students begin to knock at the door. A Year 6 student asks to speak to Sam: 'I'm very sorry Mr Hall, I won't be in my music class today because I have a violin lesson.' Sam replies, 'Thanks for letting me know.' I am quite struck by the level of courtesy shown by this young student, but the teachers are not – this is just the expectation that the school has of its students.

The enrichment programme which had brought me to the school earlier was delivered through an external provider and my contact with the regular staff while in this role was limited. However, my professional networks overlap significantly with those of the teachers at Chiswick College. I have met all of the music teachers before, and I know some quite well, through involvement in professional organisations and through common acquaintances. Sam and the other teachers speak freely in front of me – about conflicts between staff members, ongoing issues with administration – providing me with information and perspectives that an outsider would not normally be privy to. I am aware that these pre-existing relationships will affect my position as a researcher here, although I am unsure initially of how big an impact this will have on my research.

The school context

It proves very difficult to get an appointment with the Principal, Mr James Allan, so I have already observed the school and Sam's classroom for several days before we meet. As I leave the music staffroom to go to my appointment, I ask Sam and the other teachers what he is like. 'He speaks very well – it'll be a good interview', Sam tells me. I take the short walk across the manicured rose garden to the main office, where I am greeted by Mr Allan's very helpful personal assistant. I am shown through to his office. The mahogany furniture is not overly ornate, but is more luxurious than that found in other parts of the school. This room is adjacent to a major student thoroughfare, although it is quiet at the time of our meeting while the students are in class.

From what I read on the College's website, the school has a significant population of international students in the boarding house. I ask Mr Allan about the policies in place at Chiswick College regarding cultural and social inclusion, something that he seems eager to talk about.

'Chiswick College is very proud of our social inclusion, our cultural programmes, intercultural programmes … We have a very strong overseas student programme, we have done for a number of years now. We would typically have between 90 and 110 overseas girls every year. They would come from all over Asia, India, South Pacific, South America, sometimes from Europe as well, but a very strong intercultural programme of welcoming overseas students.

'More importantly during the last five or six years we've increased our Indigenous education programme and we now have 14 girls from remote Aboriginal communities who come to the College at virtually no cost to them. The College wears that cost, which is a significant financial burden to the College and it really does make me frustrated when the public say things like, you know, "private elite schools, they get all this money from the Government blah blah blah". Yet they don't realise that we're running such programmes where we are giving up a lot of income to have those girls come and live here in our boarding house, and come to school here.'

I ask about what has motivated this change in policy regarding Indigenous education: 'Are there Government directives, or does this action come from the school?'

'There are Government expectations. Certainly when I arrived in 2007 as the principal here we were asked to redress what we're providing. We had some Indigenous girls, there was a suggestion, through the Indigenous Transition Support Agencies, that we could be doing a bit more. And so the school took the initiative to increase learning support, increase personnel available to support the girls, increase monetary support as well. And so we took that view that we needed to initiate that. Now the Australian Government would expect certain things of us and they'd expect us to provide equity of access to the education, all those sort of things. But they're not driving that. It's not like they're checking what we're doing – we report back to them [on] the things that we are doing. So it's mainly school generated.'

While 14 Indigenous scholarships doesn't sound like a lot in a school of just under 1,000 students, Chiswick College's total Indigenous population (including a small number of fee-paying students whose families self-identify as being of Indigenous descent) is approximately 2 per cent. This is only slightly under the estimated percentage of the total Australian population (approximately 2.5 per cent), and is higher than all other high-fee girls' schools in metropolitan areas (Australian Curriculum Assessment and Reporting Authority, 2011).

The school recognises the need to provide extra support for these Indigenous students, particularly in the area of literacy.

'We know that we have to provide support to those people so we provide, we have Indigenous tutors who are providing learning support, we also have tutors for English as a Second Language (ESL) so that we make sure those students have the best opportunity [to succeed] at Chiswick College.'

I ask for clarification: 'When you say Indigenous tutors do you mean Indigenous people who work as tutors?'

'Yes, unfortunately we haven't been able to secure people permanently in that regard, but we have tutors who are in place for the Indigenous girls and some of those on occasions have been Indigenous people themselves. Our Year 6 teacher who is our Indigenous Liaison Officer she is Indigenous herself and so she uses her family connections and so on to help with the girls as well.

'[The Indigenous girls are] – I'm not going to use the word "assimilate".' He laughs. 'But they're a fully integrated part of ordinary, normal classes: welcomed into those classes, celebrated in those classes for the diversity they bring. I mean a quick example, an assembly we had here four or five weeks ago the Indigenous girls did a cultural dance for the students on assembly. Very warmly received, and they're the little things that help to slowly break down misunderstandings, and so we celebrate that.'

I am reminded of the description of the 'Harmony Day' celebration at St Mark's. Again, I regret that I wasn't able to attend and see this event for myself.

I ask about any additional costs that come up – uniforms, trips, extra-curricula activities that they choose to participate in: 'Does the school cover the costs of all that?'

'For the Indigenous girls, yes … We have a range of support programmes through churches and Government agencies that help to bring in little bits of income here and there. And that helps us to pay for uniforms, books, and textbooks, that sort of thing.

'We aren't like some of the high-fee schools in Brisbane, [whose families] tend to be the high-flying professionals, you know, the doctors, lawyers and those sorts of people. More of the families of Chiswick are your middle-class, everyday families, who are really spending all of their disposable income to send their children to the school and so they're very committed to [their children's] education. That makes us very aware of them and that makes us very in tune with the need to accommodate their needs, and [to provide] that equity of opportunity.'

This is reflected in the demographic data provided by the federal government. The federal government's ICSEA (Index of Community Socio-Educational Advantage) places Chiswick College with 46 per cent of students in the top quartile of household income, 31 per cent and 16 per cent in the middle quartiles, and 7 per cent in the lowest.

'We have scholarships that are available: [these are awarded in two categories], academic or excellence. Academic [scholarships are] based on an ACER (Australian Council of Educational Research) Scholarship Exam each year and we just take the top students in the results. The Excellence scholarships are based on consistent A grades in school reports or being excellent in either a sporting or a cultural activity, something like that. Then for the students from lower socio-economic backgrounds we provide a series of support encouragement bursaries. For example, a mother from the highlands of Papua New Guinea just contacted me today struggling as a single mother to keep her daughter here for Year 11 and 12 and so I've increased her support bursary ... but of course we are limited by a budget, and my school council puts pressure on me all the time to keep that down, but at the same time we're trying to help those families.'

'So I guess it's a bit of a balancing act?', I comment.

'A very big balancing act, yes.'

I'm interested to know if James, as a male Principal of an ethnically diverse school for girls, believes that there are any specific needs regarding social justice because of the student demographic.

'Possibly two things in particular. The first one is that we find that we need to work hard on developing not only that girls can achieve anything, but that girls from less fortunate communities, lower socio-economic backgrounds, culturally diverse backgrounds, we find that we have to work even harder to get them to understand and see that they have every right. For instance we've sometimes seen students from the Middle East, girls from the Middle East who have been very suppressed in the past, and we need to bring them out of that and [to encourage] them to strive, to ask and to expect, and to try – those sort of things. With the Indigenous girls we first of all need to raise their self-esteem, that's very, very important for those girls.'

While Chiswick College's Indigenous scholarship programme is certainly not solving the problems of Indigenous education, it provides opportunities for Indigenous girls who otherwise may not aspire to complete their secondary education.

James continues. 'But the other thing we need to work very hard on, and it'll be an ongoing problem, is there is too much social or racial stereotyping from the community and wider. For instance we have boarding parents from western country Queensland and New South Wales who do not like having overseas students in the school, do not like having Indigenous students in the school, refer to them as "them", "those students", you know, that sort of thing. This is where our school tries very hard to educate our parents about those things and that's why every time we celebrate the diversity, the cultural, the Indigenous, we celebrate very hard because we want our parents to get the message that "we know you have a point of view, we know that your point of view is very racist and we're not going to accept that in our school".'

I ask James if he can provide an example to illustrate what he means.

'Invariably, they're parents of boarders who contact me by phone, telling me about something that has happened in the boarding house between their daughter and another one of the girls. Something like swearing; one of "those girls" has sworn at their daughter. When they say this to me, and I ask them "one of which girls?", I get "you know, one of those black girls" as a reply. And I say to the parent "Do you think that's an appropriate way to speak about this student?" It's common for these parents to refer to Indigenous or Asian students as a collective. We do have to remember that these are often parents from very isolated rural communities, where there are deep-seated racial stereotypes, but it's not an attitude that we're willing to accept.'

As a school with a high level of cultural diversity, values of tolerance and respect are embedded within the College's ethos. Mr Allan seems to recognise that there are many within the school community who are marginalised in various ways – women and girls, Indigenous students and their families, ESL students, rural students, students from developing countries. At times, the action taken may skim the surface of the real issues – e.g. cultural dance displays as a means of breaking down cultural barriers – while at other times the measures seem to promote understanding between members of the school community. I wonder, however, how deeply this intolerance of racism permeates the values of the school, whether it is limited to a rejection of overt acts of discrimination or whether it extends to a challenge of hegemony at an institutional level.

At a later time, James reads this and asks me about this last sentence.

'Good question', he says, 'I assume that what you're asking is do we go out of our way?'

I am again reminded that I need to take off my 'academic hat', that institutional v. interpersonal racism and hegemonic values aren't concepts that are commonly discussed by people outside of academia, even amongst the highly educated. I attempt to describe what I mean.

'Most Australians reject notions of overt racial discrimination: refusing to speak to or work with someone because of the colour of their skin, hurtful name-calling, things like that. However, we continue to hear people say "I'm not a racist ..."'

'I'm not a racist, but ...', James finishes my thought for me. 'Yes, I understand where you're coming from; you're asking "Do we go out of our way to value what these students bring to our school." I would hope that our teachers are moving from "dealing with" Indigenous girls in their classes and moving towards "How can I find out more about this student and incorporate that into my classroom?" One of our ESL teachers has really gone out of her way to learn about the Indigenous students we have here and incorporate more culturally relevant materials into their literacy support: I think there's a big spectrum of attitudes amongst the teaching staff, I've told you what I would hope for from our staff, but I know that some of them aren't there yet. It's a long process.'

Throughout my visits to Chiswick College, I notice a sense of academic competitiveness, a sense of striving for academic excellence from the girls. In one of the lessons I observe, a Year 12 student asks her teacher 'I'm happy with my mark (an A), but what would I have needed to do to get a better mark? Did anyone get an A+?' I ask James about this.

'I think the second phrase you used was probably the more apt ... that we strive for personal academic excellence. We place a lot of emphasis on "value-added education" here – some other high-fee schools may only concentrate on the academic [aspects of education]. Whereas we say "we don't care about students getting As". [If they do,] that's good and we'll celebrate that, but the student who raises from a D to a B, or a D to a C, or a C to a B – whatever. That's what we celebrate in this school. For instance, one of our Indigenous girls who came last year who was below the NAPLAN [National Assessment Programme – Literacy and Numeracy] benchmarks, is now achieving at a solid C and B level in her subjects ... They're the things that we celebrate as a staff. So in terms of what's important to us about academic achievement, it's every student at every level and the best that they can be personally.'

As I leave James' office to return to the music staffroom, I reflect upon what we discussed. The school's supportive approach to each girl's development, the presence of an Indigenous scholarship programme and the willingness of the principal to stand up to fee-paying parents who hold racially inappropriate views is something I was not expecting to see in a school such as this. I am interested to see how the values that James has described are lived out and experienced by the teachers and students. In some ways, I feel as if I've just been given a sales pitch, a very good one: his ability to articulate his ideas so eloquently presents a convincing argument. James says to me later that he hopes I don't really think that. 'I have a genuine passion for this school and what we're trying to do here. I'm not trying to sell it to you, to present a view that is unrealistic, but I welcomed the chance to share with you the vision that I have for Chiswick College.'

Introducing Sam Hall

Sam is 25 years old and is in his third year of teaching at Chiswick College. Sam takes a rather casual attitude to conducting our first interview, which takes place during the lunch break on the first day of my observations. We begin by searching the school for an empty classroom to use. Because it is lunchtime, we are interrupted every few minutes by a loudspeaker delivering messages to the students. After around 20 minutes we are required to vacate that room for a waiting class and we head off again to find an available room.

After we eventually get settled, I ask Sam to tell me about his experiences as a music student.

'I grew up in Eumundi on the Sunshine Coast and moved to Brisbane to study at university when I was 17. While I was at school, my piano teacher was an ex-policeman who didn't really play the piano that well but preferred teaching to the work of a policeman. My experience of music in school mostly comprised participating in ensembles and musicals, which offered me a far more rich and rewarding experience than was offered in my individual piano lessons. It gave me an opportunity to perform with others, to make mistakes in public and to be offered an introduction to a variety of different styles of music.

'When I think back to my classroom music experience I see that most of what we studied was in preparation for assessment: many different "units" of work, without an underlying sequence or progression. Most of what I did was to prepare for upcoming assessment. For example, if the class had a composition due, our lessons would be spent composing for that particular task. If we had an exam soon, our lessons would be spent analysing the pieces in the upcoming exam. Rehearsals for upcoming performances were also a large part of lesson time: I remember playing the piano a lot, picking up guitars and playing the drums. One thing I now find interesting is that we only learned sol-fa briefly, when practising for melodic dictation exams. My teacher tried to prepare these skills but I think it was difficult for her to do so: how to be successful in dictation.'

Sam has a very clear agenda here. I realise as soon as he begins to speak that he is distancing his own high school experience from the way he teaches. I ask Sam to elaborate on how his experience of music at school differs from his teaching approach.

'I see now that one very important factor in conveying musical knowledge is structure: sequence and progression. With this in place immediately concepts appear in context – clearly connected to one another – and structured so that the connections between them are more easily grasped. I am concerned that offering students an introduction to a variety of musical experiences only offers a glimpse of different genres, practices, concepts without offering a solid, connected platform for understanding or a depth of knowledge in those areas. I certainly believe that it is important to experience music of different styles, but not completely at the expense of theoretical musical understanding. I also believe that the teaching of sol-fa is paramount to the development of critical listening skills, reading and writing skills and composition skills. My own growth as a musician rapidly increased when sol-fa was introduced to me later in life, at university. In comparison to how I learned at school, I can see that there was a lack of structure and almost a complete lack of group singing, which I now view (only in retrospect) as a serious downfall.'

I ask Sam about how he came to consider a musical career, and specifically as a music teacher.

'I am a very indecisive person. I suppose in the end I just kind of fell into pursuing a musical career because I found it hard to make a decision. I had achieved quite well in a number of areas but couldn't decide which I enjoyed more. It was when, in Year 11, I began to achieve well in music that I first considered possibly following a career in it. I originally enrolled in a dual degree programme – Bachelor of Arts/Bachelor of Education – but I didn't complete the Bachelor of Education, still unsure about becoming a teacher in my fourth year at university. I graduated with a Bachelor of Arts and then decided to complete a Graduate Diploma in Education.'

I ask Sam if he can recall an experience of feeling excluded from music or music education.

'The most vivid feeling of exclusion that comes to mind is my experience of auditioning for university. Obviously, the standards that are applied are very, very high, but I had very little instrumental experience. When I look back, I think my musical understanding and my experience at performing was actually quite advanced, it just didn't sort of marry up with my technical ability on the piano. In my audition I was challenged and asked whether or not I practised for four hours a day, to which I responded, "No, no one's ever told me I had to, what are you talking about?"'

I get the impression that Sam didn't think much of his own music education; that he feels that he missed out on valuable learning experiences that would have benefited him, both in classroom music and in his instrumental learning. In a later conversation, I ask Sam whether he agrees with my observation.

'Yes, absolutely. What I naturally had as a student was creativity and "musicality", which was encouraged by my teachers but not nurtured or developed into real musical knowledge and skills. Therefore, my creativity and musicality could only develop as far as my limited technical ability would allow. I ensure now that my students work hard to develop strong technical abilities, which will enhance and strengthen their creative expression.'

Sam's values and beliefs about music education

The way Sam teaches music now is vastly different from the way he was taught, a phenomenon that some suggest is unusual for teachers (Richardson, 1996, 2003). I ask him what he believes is the most important aspect of his classroom teaching.

'Performing, singing, being a part of music making every lesson. I believe that if you can get up in front of a bunch of people and sing confidently, then you can get up in front of a bunch of people and you can deliver a convincing argument – you can sell your ideas and you can sell yourself as a person, and for life, I believe that is important. I really want my students to be able to develop the confidence to just sing in front of one another. The programme here at this school is excellent at addressing that because we do it every lesson. Also, I believe it is important to develop theoretical musical knowledge, which the students learn here through a performance-based programme.'

Sam's own relaxed but confident manner is one of the first things I noticed during my observations. Despite being a young, quite inexperienced teacher, he doesn't seem fazed having a researcher follow him around and watch his lessons. In fact, very little seems to faze Sam.

Sam continues. 'I worry that a lot of programmes that teach songs and teach pieces rather than teaching "music" only teach the students to learn how to play that piece really, really well, but then they're not actually given any knowledge that provides them with the ability to go out and apply that to music in an unknown context.'

'So it's not developing transferrable skills?', I suggest.

'Exactly – it's just "do this". As a child I always wanted to learn the piano piece that looked the most impressive. It didn't matter to me that I wasn't learning anything about music as long as my fingers could play it. I was a terrible, terrible sight-reader, because I hadn't learned those skills. I hadn't learned about the theory of music. I knew nothing about key signatures. I just thought that they were there and I could ignore them and I probably wouldn't even know the difference. Now I believe that embedding that [theoretical] knowledge into the students' education is paramount because it enables them to [engage with] music much more knowingly.

'I believe that being a musician isn't something that is arcane; it's not something that only a few, "talented" people can be and I am concerned that we live in a culture where you have to be able to play a violin sonata for somebody to consider you a "real musician" and it is just ridiculous for us to be thinking that way because how many people even observe those sorts of experiences? Very few people go to classical concerts. The music that is a part of their lives is singing in the shower or listening to a piece of music on the radio. By teaching music to everyone, we help them to understand the music in their lives a little more deeply and enable them to listen in an informed way and with a broadened platform of understanding.

'What I want is to give the students the skills to continue making music after they finish school. I would hate to think that the students that go on to study medicine or study to become a vet or become a chef, don't continue to love and to seek out musical experiences. I believe that it is much more difficult for them to do that if they perceive it to be difficult or unachievable.'

Sam's desire to avoid positioning music as arcane suggests that he wants to make music real for the students, to connect with their musical experiences and provide them with something that enriches their lives. I am interested to see how this plays out in practice.

Music at Chiswick College

The music programme at Chiswick College has a very strong tradition in music education underpinned by the Kodály philosophy. In the late 1970s, Chiswick was one of the first schools in Queensland to implement daily music lessons with a specialist teacher in the junior school, a programme that continues today. There is a sense of a 'united front' across the music programme at the College – there is a work programme for Prep to Year 12 that outlines the content that is expected to be covered in each year, focusing on the development of aural skills through singing in sol-fa. This knowledge is drawn upon in the substantial choral programme. Sam was recruited as a graduate for his position because of the close alignment between the school's methodological approach and his preservice training at university.

While teachers have the opportunity to be flexible and responsive within the framework of 'the programme', the history of the programme positions musical knowledge and pedagogy as somewhat fixed, as something that transcends the teacher and students.

Year 8 music at Chiswick: 'Right back to the start'

Like most P-12 schools in Queensland, Chiswick College has several 'intakes', a point where they increase the size of the student cohort. At Chiswick, major intakes happen in Year 5 and Year 8. I ask Sam to tell me about how he plans for classes where new students join with others who have been studying a sequential programme.

'Well, the perfect example is Year 8 music where we have students who've come through the Chiswick College music programme – and by the time they're in Year 7 they understand major and minor scales, mixed metres, heaps of others stuff, and they're doing it well. They go into Year 8 music and they will start again because we get a huge amount of students in from other schools who have had varied or no musical backgrounds at all. So for Year 8 music we go right back to the start.

'This enables us to make sure that all of the kids [from other schools] who haven't learned anything aren't left by the wayside. Also, the girls do 13 subjects in Grade 8 or the entire year here at Chiswick, so that's another issue that we have to be aware of. Making things simple in Year 8 music is a good way to make sure that everyone comes on board.

'However, we try to extend the ones who've done it all before – we can teach a piece of music and have some students singing it in unison, we can have the students who need a challenge singing it in three-part canon in small groups. We can be asking our students to write three notes out in doh = F, but we can then ask the students who've had background in music to write it out in any number of keys. I think the idea is that the concepts, across the board, are quite basic, but there's room for extension.'

Sam's classroom

Most of the lessons I observe over the course of my research take a similar format – the students work as a whole class, either seated at their desks or standing in the large open space at the back of the room. The students sing a series of songs throughout the lesson, with the singing leading to part singing, analysis, staff writing, recorder and keyboard performance, or a movement or clapping game.

In Sam's classroom, the teacher is positioned as the holder of knowledge. In the case of an analysis activity, students sing the song – most often a folk song or canon from a Western tradition – before being guided through the deconstruction: how many sounds on this beat? Were they even or uneven? Who can describe the lengths of the sounds using long and short? Many of Sam's questions to the class are very specifically worded, and he clearly has a very specific answer in mind. At times students give answers that are outside the acceptable range – Sam then provides prompts to guide the student to give the answer he wants.

'Wrong and strong': creating a risk-taking classroom

Because Sam's classroom (and indeed the classroom music programme from Prep to Year 12 at Chiswick College) is so heavily based on the students learning through singing, he recognises the importance of creating a safe classroom environment, one in which students support each other and can make mistakes without fear of ridicule.

'For me, addressing the students' confidence issues in terms of singing is important. For example, a Year 10 student who joined music this year is very shy and, understandably, finds it difficult to perform with the class – and joining Year 10 music at Chiswick is challenging if you have never studied music theory before. For me it has been about trying to open her up to the classroom ethos, which is that we can sing and make mistakes and do stupid things in front of each other and we're not going to judge one another. And I do have this conversation with all of my classes throughout the year because as much as you talk about it some of them still struggle.

'I see myself as a good model for them because I often get up and make mistakes. My voice breaks every five minutes if I haven't warmed up properly. I like that they can see that I can get up there and do that, and I can still get on with my life. It doesn't affect me so gravely that I have to go back to my staffroom and cry – it just happens. And it happens all the time, you know, you can go and see the most proficient and accomplished musicians and they're still going to make mistakes. It's having the resilience to deal with it, I guess, that I want to start to embed in these students now, because performance is a huge part of what they do in the music classroom.

'Towards the end of my degree, I joined a choir that performed quite regularly and that helped me to develop more confidence. I think that has sort of seeped out into other parts of my life. I really want my students to be able to develop the confidence to just sing in front of one another.'

I ask Sam how he goes about encouraging the students to support one another in the classroom, and how he responds if they aren't doing so.

'To me, to be honest, I find that really difficult. As much as I can, I try to encourage an environment where everyone feels comfortable with one another, but I find it hard to reprimand students for doing the wrong thing, without making everyone in the classroom feel uncomfortable about it. So if somebody just, offhand, says, you know, "oh, that was pathetic", or "that was so wrong", and has a laugh about it, I find it difficult to address that in the classroom without making everyone think, "oh, now we all feel uncomfortable".'

During my observations, I notice that Sam appears to do a very good job at avoiding this type of behaviour, by calling on students who he thinks will be successful at the performance tasks, by offering support to those students who he thinks will need it. At no time do I observe an instance of a student being asked to perform individually and failing.

Building relationships

Over the course of my observations, it becomes clear to me that Sam is a teacher who is well liked by the students and staff. One of my observation days falls on the day after the sports carnival, where, based on the students' retelling, Sam led his house's cheer squad in renditions of 'YMCA' and 'The Nutbush', and running a relay leg for the team that didn't have enough runners. His interactions with the students are relaxed and friendly, often spending time chatting with individuals before the lesson begins. When the girls became chatty or off-task during lessons or rehearsals he simply begins singing the next song; invariably the students join in quickly, thus avoiding any need for confrontation. Of course, the girls' compliant behaviour and good manners mean that I never actually see a reason for Sam to take a more assertive approach.

'I feel that I know some of my students very, very well – I've taught some of them for a few years, and I see some of them for choir or piano lessons. So I think even I have those sorts of conversations with my students where it's almost friendly. It's sort of "out of the classroom banter" but it's happening in the classroom and I fear that sometimes there is too much familiarity, especially for students who are looking in from the outside of that relationship, but I think the solution for that is to make everyone feel comfortable and for me to get to know my students as much as I possibly can. I really think that just being a bit friendly and a bit personable with students is a really good way to make a connection and to ultimately make them feel comfortable in your classroom and be successful.

'I had been on Year 10 camp at the start of last term with all of the Year 10 students, but three of the girls from my music class were in my group – two of the Indigenous girls and Mary from Papua New Guinea – and I had a great time with them. We just laughed and made jokes, had a hilarious time, and I think they really sought that friendly, big-brother relationship with me because they were out in the middle of nowhere, and it was raining and all sorts of things were going on – everyone was covered in leeches! However, I observed that it was difficult for them to then bring our relationship back into the classroom, without the constant distraction of friendly banter and story-telling. It is quite easy for me because I'm a teacher: I can come into the classroom and I can be nasty, I can be strict, I can do all of the "teacher" things that I need to do, because I've got a class in front of me and I have a job to do.'

'Nasty and strict doesn't really sound like you though', I say to Sam.

'I suppose I expect the classroom to be managed in a certain way: silence when I am speaking, listening from all of the students and "having a go". As I described earlier, I believe that a successful music classroom has a great deal of structure. When the students don't observe the structure I respond by speaking to them about appropriate behaviour, and ultimately, when that behaviour is not corrected, I introduce disciplinary measures like separating students and detentions. While this may not seem like "being mean or nasty", it feels that way to me. I feel as though I am, to some degree, sabotaging the relationship I have built with the students outside of the classroom: I have allowed them to engage with me on a more social level in one instance, and then I am denying them that right in the classroom. I have found it difficult to integrate that friendliness in the structure of the classroom. For the two Indigenous students, it was really hard for them to forget the experience that we'd had on camp and just to get on with things and get work done.'

Some time later, I ask Sam to revisit this. I ask, 'Do you think they really needed to forget this? It almost contradicts what you'd said earlier about needing to form a relationship with the students.'

'"To forget this" is a poor way to communicate what I mean. I need them to honour their responsibility in the classroom and see that our relationship in the classroom is built on a necessity to achieve certain tasks and follow procedures. I have spoken to them explicitly about this, but distraction seems a more attractive alternative to the classes I have planned. The question I ask myself now is: how do I achieve what I believe to be integral in planning a successful music classroom while maintaining a friendly, casual relationship with the students. I have seen that they respond well in the context of our "non-classroom" relationship but I don't feel as though I can teach them what I believe is important for them to learn if they don't obey the classroom rules and temporarily put aside the memories of Year 10 camp. For me (and for the students who have studied at this college for many years already) the expectations in my classroom are clear. For the newcomers, however, they have to learn them.'

Year 10 music: 'About as diverse as you get here'

As Sam and I walk to his classroom after morning tea, he describes the Year 10 class that I am about to meet for the first time – the very diverse class that he has referred to several times in our interviews and conversations. 'There are two Indigenous scholarship students in the class, one who started at Chiswick College at the start of this year, and one who came in at the end of last year. There is another student from Papua New Guinea who started this year, as well as another girl who came from another school, who is quite musical, but hasn't done theory before. These students all really struggle to keep up. There's usually anywhere between 9 and 13 students in this class, depends on the day.'

I find this somewhat surprising – truancy doesn't seem like it would be easy to get away with at Chiswick College. Sam explains to me the reasons why some of the students aren't in class all the time.

'Some of the students had been undergoing ESL support lessons which occurred during music and some had also been granted time to sit quietly in the library and study on their core subjects during this time. I had communicated with the administration at the school about this and they had decided that extra support, in terms of time, was needed for particularly the Indigenous students who were having some trouble transitioning into the school and that affected their participation in this class.'

I am interested to see how Sam works with students with such disparate levels of knowledge and experience. 'My lesson plan varies depending on who is here – if the new ones are here it's revision, if they're not, we might go on.'

Today the majority of the students are here and the lesson begins in typical fashion – singing as a class. The difference between the students' level of experience is obvious immediately. Around two-thirds of the students participate confidently, while the others are hesitant. Sam encourages everyone to sing out, avoiding singling out particular students. The singing moves on seamlessly to writing out the same song in staff notation. Sam tours the class as the students do this, offering assistance to students who need it. After seeing that a few of the students have completed the task quickly, he asks all students to pause for a moment while he explains the extension task – all students then continue working at their own pace. The students are expected to work individually, and they don't really interact with each other unless they are talking quietly because they are finished.

Several students are reluctant to continue with the task without Sam watching over them and talking them through what to do. Sam describes that he finds this frustrating. 'I've offered them extra tutorials at lunchtimes but they haven't taken me up on it.'

'Music for all' is the underlying stated philosophy of the programme at Chiswick College, and, certainly, no student is stopped from enrolling in classroom music because of a lack of prior experience. The school typically has between 15 and 20 per cent of the Senior cohort taking classroom music – a slightly higher-than-average rate of participation, but not altogether unusual given the school's middle-/upper-middle-class clientele. However, watching this class, it is clear that not all students are going to be successful. The students who have been studying music at Chiswick since Year 8 (or earlier) have developed insider knowledge – capital – in the form of language, knowledge and skills that are a prerequisite for success.

A few days later, I observe another lesson with the same class. As we walk to the classroom, Sam advises me that this lesson will be a bit of a break from the normal routine – it is the students' last lesson of the term and there will be several students missing because of a choral workshop. The lesson begins with quite a long chat session while they wait for other students to arrive. I notice that this type of relaxed conversation also develops the relationship between the students, helping the newer students to feel more relaxed among their more musically experienced peers.

While reminiscing about their adventures several months prior on Year 10 camp, the two Indigenous students tell stories of their interactions with Sam. "Member on that hike, in the rain, when Mr Hall let me wear his shoes? My feet were killin', 'cos mine were too small, so he swapped with me', Sharnee says.

As the stories continue, Sam turns to me and says with a smile, 'On camp they were teaching me their lingo.' Karla interrupts with a word from her first language – 'You remember? Bonboyana' – to which Sam responds, jokingly 'And now she's swearing at me!' Karla repeats, putting her fist on her chest 'Bonboyana', she says again, 'it means "between us"'. Sam repeats the word 'Bonboyana – I love learning new things'. I can't help but wonder to myself whether Karla is reminding her teacher of the vocabulary he learned on camp or if she is cautioning her teacher not to say too much to the others, to keep their experience 'between us'.

This discussion gradually dies down as it is accepted that no other students will arrive. Sam introduces the task for today – Year 10 Music Trivia. Sam has prepared a series of questions and tasks for the students to complete, working in teams that he has chosen. Sam has deliberately chosen heterogeneous groups for the students to work in, pairing weaker students with stronger. I ask Sam why he chose to have the students work in these groups: 'Basically, because some of the students in that class wouldn't have been able to answer a single question.'

Sam explains the only rule of the game: that the group members have to work together and each person has to contribute. The group that is seated nearest to me is the one that I have the opportunity to observe closely. One of the group's members, Rebecca, a student who has been at Chiswick College since Prep, is currently the top student in this class. She is fiercely competitive and takes a natural leadership role within the group, discussing the questions (and her answers) with the two weaker members of the group, Jess and Mary. I see Rebecca begin to take on a peer-teaching role. One of the tasks is to write one of their known songs in staff notation. Rather than complete this herself, a task that she could complete quickly and accurately, she guides Mary while she writes out the song, carefully looking over her shoulder, prompting Mary with questions when she is about to go wrong. Rebecca's verbal explanations are clear and concise; she frequently sings the relevant part of the song to help Mary make the connection between sound and symbol, in much the same way that Sam does in his lessons. After ten years of music lessons at Chiswick College, Rebecca is adept at utilising the pedagogical techniques of her teachers. With Rebecca's assistance, Mary completes the task successfully and wins the points for her team. (None of the students seem to mind that there is no prize – winning seems to be reward enough.) High-fives are exchanged and Mary's smile lights up the room. I wonder if this is the first time she has experienced any success in the music classroom.

While I observe this powerful example of peer mentoring, I recall Sam's earlier comments to me that Mary is one of the students he has been encouraging to come and see him for extra help, but she hasn't done so thus far. I wonder if Mary would be more inclined to work with another student. I ask Sam about this.

'I had offered all of the new students this year the opportunity to participate in a peer-mentoring programme that the school offers. Sadly, while some of the existing students in the class were quite enthusiastic, the new students weren't. I wonder if they were too shy and self-conscious in the early stages at the College to agree to it.'

This lesson is markedly different from all of the other lessons I have observed Sam teach. For the first time, I have seen students sharing their knowledge with each other, allowing stronger students in the class to take the role of expert.

Later, I discuss this lesson with Sam at length.

'I think one of the wonderful things about being at the top end of understanding, as in being somebody that understands things well, and grasps things quickly … is that you can practise and consolidate that even more by teaching it to people who don't understand. For me as a teacher I've had so many moments where I've finally understood things just because I had to break it down and explain it to somebody who didn't understand, and, similarly, the students in the class who think they already know it can have the opportunity to practise and to share and hopefully consolidate those understandings for themselves by explaining it to the students in the class who don't really understand what's going on, or have less understanding. In turn, for the students with less understanding, they have the opportunity to learn from their peers, which I think is pretty special. While I try to explain concepts clearly, I do forget that the musical language I use is quite sophisticated as a result of the way that I've been taught and the words that now come out of my mouth. Students in the class who don't understand sometimes just don't get it, but they don't put their hand up and say they don't get it because they're in what they think is a classroom full of people who do get it. In that sense, when they're in a smaller group, too, they'll feel more comfortable tapping another person on the shoulder and saying "Hey, look, there's only two others of you here so I can ask this. I'm not going to ask in front of the class because that's too embarrassing, but what does this mean and can you explain it to me?"'

About six months after this observation, I ask Sam about how this class is going.

'The class has changed significantly since last term. One of our indigenous students (Sharnee) has gone back to Weipa.'

I feel slightly saddened to hear this. I ask Sam if he knows why.

'Not entirely. I know that Sharnee and Karla are cousins, and they had been best mates when they were back in their hometown but Karla had been putting in a concerted effort to achieve well at Chiswick for six months prior to Sharnee arriving. When Sharnee arrived, things changed dramatically for Karla and she lost a lot of motivation and her attitude declined rapidly. There was a lot of pairing up of those two that Karla didn't like. She had felt that she had made a go of it in this new environment and she wanted to keep going with that and I think she also felt a little self-conscious that she was doing that in front of somebody from her hometown who ultimately would've judged her for changing her ways. I think their relationship just wasn't good at all and so it was a mutual decision by Sharnee's parents and the school to send her back home, but Karla has stayed on.

I had a parent–teacher interview with Karla and her mum – she hadn't achieved very well in music at all: she'd just scraped through on a very generous pass from her music teacher. I spoke to her mother, who wasn't impressed that Karla wasn't motivated to do any work and she, the mother, put that down to music being a subject that she just shouldn't be doing because it's "airy fairy" and it's not good for her anyway. I simply put it down to a lack of motivation that I assumed was across all of Karla's subjects. I could be wrong, I still don't know. So, in the end, Karla left the subject on the advice of her mother.

'And then there's Mary, from Papua New Guinea. I think Mary is an example of a student who is quite capable but has absolutely no confidence in music whatsoever and I think had, in that quiz lesson alone, a few "light-bulb moments", where she finally made connections that she just didn't get before and there are so many of those connections for her to make before she reaches the same level as the rest of the class. She came back after the holidays to see me and in the first lesson said to me, "OK, Mr Hall. I'm finally starting to understand this, I need to see you on Friday afternoons for half an hour after school because I really wanna improve." And I think that lesson was sort of a light-at-the-end-of-the-tunnel moment for her and she thought, "Oh, OK. I can get there."'

'And has she come to see you?', I ask, recalling our earlier conversations about Mary's reluctance to ask for help.

'Yes, she has on a number of occasions. She's improving, oh my goodness. The composition that she just handed in was spectacular. She admitted to having help but she sought that help herself, which might have been because she'd had the experience in the classroom that left her feeling confident enough to ask other people to help. I don't know for sure, but it's possible.'

This help that she sought was from her classmates, something that I can't picture the Mary I had seen earlier in the year doing. The 'light-bulb moments' that took place in that lesson were more than just increasing her level of understanding – the fact that she shared them with Rebecca made a social connection with the class that had not existed before. The relevance of Sam's comments regarding the need for a supportive classroom environment conducive to risk taking and the importance of relationships between teacher and student and between the students can be seen in the development of this one student, and how this single learning event changed the way she experienced the music classroom.

Later, Sam emails me with an update regarding Mary's progress.

'There is a lovely story here, Rachael. Mary achieved an A grade at the end of the year – combining her rapidly improving theoretical knowledge, her strong natural singing abilities and her successful composition task. She also joined the school choir! At the end of the year her mother wrote me an email thanking me for supporting her daughter, "so far away in another country" and shared her happiness at seeing her daughter enjoying and achieving well in music. It was a rewarding email to receive.'

Sam continues, telling me about another student who had left the class. 'Another student, Jess, had come from another school at the start of the year. Jess didn't like that she was – I don't want to say forced – but regularly encouraged to sing. That made her feel very uncomfortable despite doing very well at it, and I continued to praise her for the efforts that she was making. I thought that I'd tried to make her comfortable but that is a process that can take some time, and in the end I respect that she didn't want to join in. At her old school, Jess's experience in music had been similar to my own: pick to up a guitar and learn to play chords in the classroom and she had loved that in the past and I just don't do that in my classroom. I think there's room for it, and I would like to make room for it because, to be honest, that was a large part of my own musical education and here I am. It often involved just working things out for yourself. I believe that there is merit in this, but first I wish to impart knowledge and skills that students can then go away and practise, improvise with and consolidate.'

I ask Sam why he hasn't made room for this type of learning in the past.

'I fear that those experiences aren't what students "need" in the classroom. I suppose I have a very focused and specific idea about how a music classroom should be, based on my own [teaching] experience and my training. It doesn't fit in with the "perfect model" I have in my mind and so I am reluctant to try it.

'I'd spent the whole of first semester encouraging her to stay with it, and she was achieving quite well, sitting on a B, which is a high achievement for somebody who's come into Year 10 music with the inability to read staff notation. I mean, there are many positives: she left [the subject] knowing how to read the treble clef, which she didn't know how to do when she came in. She left with an understanding of how rhythm works and she hadn't in the past.'

Sam reflects on this story sometime later. 'I read this and I think to myself: where is the consideration for her simply enjoying herself in the classroom? Where have I tried to make an effort for her to have a little of what she was used to in my classroom? While I was encouraging and sympathetic to her concerns, I didn't change the way I taught: that seems like a failure to offer her an opportunity that could have flourished.'

I ask Sam to think about how he would answer the questions he poses. He says he'll keep thinking and get back to me. I remain in contact with him, but he doesn't have the answers before this manuscript is published. Sam's journey isn't bound by my research deadlines.

Mary and Jess are both students who like music and have some experience in music learning, although in a very different context. From the time they joined this music class at Chiswick College in Year 10 they have been encouraged to 'get with the programme' – gently pushed into becoming a part of the culture of learning in this way by participating in these ways of music making. Immediate success is not mandatory or expected, but immediate participation is. The pressure to conform (or perhaps assimilate …) is immense, yet unstated.

Isabel's story

Isabel Kang is a student in Sam's Year 12 class. When Sam asks her to be interviewed for my study she seems interested and pleased to be invited. I have observed Isabel in Sam's class and she immediately stands out as one of the strongest students. She participates confidently and enthusiastically, very much a part of the group.

On the day of our interview appointment, Isabel brings me the consent forms – signed by her and her parents. I notice that her father's signature is written in an Asian script so I ask her whether her parents speak and can read English, not wanting to be caught without adequate informed consent. She assures me that she translated the paperwork for her parents – I can only imagine that Isabel must have to do this a lot. Throughout our interview, Isabel frequently pauses after I have asked a question, carefully considering her words before she begins to speak. Her spoken English is not perfect, but she has an extensive vocabulary that allows her to express herself clearly and articulately.

Isabel tells me that she was born in Korea, where she lived until immigrating to Australia with her family when she was 12. She describes some of the difficulties she had when she first began school at Chiswick College, shortly after her arrival in Australia.

'Like, the culture was very – not very – but slightly different so I found it even difficult to speak to the teachers. Because in Korea it's rude to speak eye-to-eye with teachers, but when I came here, you know how we have to speak eye-to-eye? So, I didn't do that and the teacher got very angry with me … So he was "Oh, why aren't you like looking at me?" and I was like "Oh, I'm sorry I didn't know that."' Isabel laughs at the memory of her misunderstanding.

'So it took a while to get used to?', I ask.

'Yeah. But it's much better now than I first came here, yeah.'

Isabel tells me that she has only just started doing classroom music again, that she had too many other subjects she wanted to do in Years 9, 10 and 11 that she couldn't fit music in. 'I didn't choose music, just because … I'm doing music outside as well … so I was like, "Oh, I can do music outside school, but I can't do this subject outside of the school."'

I ask her why she decided to return to classroom music in Year 12.

'Because … the first reason is because I have fun in music, rather than the other subjects. Other subjects I have to concentrate, I have to pay a lot of attention to it, but in music I have freedom.'

I try to get Isabel to explain this a little more. 'Do you mean it's not as academic?', I prompt.

'It's kind of academic, it's something that I enjoy a lot so it gives me more freedom … For example in maths you know you have to concentrate a lot, but in music it's more … you can still concentrate even though we like talking to others like we are all … oh, it's hard to explain but … It's different to other subjects, yeah.'

I ask Isabel to tell me about her favourite things about classroom music.

'We can talk and we can discuss with each other … and we sing and we play different instruments … And when you sing you have to think about it … the pitch and everything, but like you don't have to be stressed, you know? And it's like music – it makes people happy I think, so when we sing together it gives me … releases all the stress.

'But composing – that's the best part … I love composition … I love the challenge of it and I love when I add the instruments each time, like "Oh, I can do this, I can do this" … like, when I compose all the things I feel like I'm good at music. We just had the composition task … When I finished that task I was like "Wow, this music is really pretty, so I can make pretty music even though I'm a real, I'm not a real composer." I felt really successful and happy about it.'

'How did you develop the skills to create that music, to compose? Where did you learn them?', I ask.

'Like, our music teacher, Mr Hall, he told us how to do it and he figured out that I have the perfect pitch – I didn't know that!' Isabel laughs. 'But I was like, yeah, it was easy for me to compose it.'

We talk for a while longer. As I move to end the interview, I ask Isabel if she has anything else that she would like to add, if there's anything she thinks I should have asked her but didn't.

'The one thing I really quickly want to say I was …'. Isabel pauses. 'You know how in Korea or in Asia country we have all different, like different, like traditional instruments?'

'Yes', I say.

'I was sad that they really didn't have it here like in Western countries … Like we have that [Western instruments] in Korea but you don't … Australia doesn't have the Korean traditional instruments.'

'So you haven't seen any here? Did you play an instrument in Korea?', I ask.

'Yes', Isabel replies. 'Yep ... It was traditional recorder. It's similar to flute but it's a kind of recorder. It sounds very traditional as in like ...' Isabel's voice trails off. Despite her success in classroom music at Chiswick College she does not have the words to describe the timbre of her instrument. I ask Isabel what the instrument is called.

'It's called "danso". It's made from wood and it's like wooden flute but in vertical position ... And there's another instrument – a string instrument sounds, very beautiful, it's very expensive but it's really beautiful and it sounds, it's similar as harp but it makes different quality of sound.'

'And so you would like to be able to play one of those instruments here if you could?' Isabel doesn't really answer my question, but her response draws my attention to the reason that she wants to talk about this.

'Like, if I see like the Australian students playing that instruments ... I would think "Oh, the world is [becoming] one" ... It's very ... we see people like Asian people playing flute and like violin and like Western instruments but we don't see many Australian people playing the Korean traditional instruments.'

'Have you ever listened to any Korean music at school? Have you been asked about, or have you ever talked to anyone about instruments and music in Korea?', I ask.

'Not really, no.'

'I think that would be something really interesting for you to share with your music teachers and peers', I tell Isabel, in the hope that she may summon the courage to do this without her teachers' prompting.

'Well, that was all.' Isabel signals that she has nothing more to say.

Isabel's story of participating in classroom music at Chiswick College, and indeed her participation in Western music making more broadly, is one that is coloured by contradictions. It is clear from the way Isabel talks about music that music making, especially composition, is something that she loves. As an intelligent, studious, high-achieving student, music provides a release, a sense of freedom, something that she doesn't experience in her other subjects. However, the cultural tensions that emerge from Isabel's narration of her experience of classroom music draw attention to the ways in which music teachers may silence their students' musical heritage through their assumptions. Because Isabel has knowledge and experience of Western music, she achieves highly in classroom music. In this classroom, her skills in performing Korean music are of no benefit, and she has not been given the opportunity to explore or share this in the music classroom.

I carefully start to explore some of these ideas with Sam. At the time that Sam and I are discussing this, he is still Isabel's teacher, so for now at least, my questions are general and non-specific. I begin by asking Sam about the high number of students from Asia at Chiswick College. 'Have you had any students come who were very new arrivals to Australia? Have you had them come into your classes?'

'None of them come into the classroom without going through the International College (a specialist ESL college affiliated with the school). So the process there is for them to spend some time sort of, integrating, assimilating maybe, even.'

Sam seems to hesitate here. I am reminded of Mr Allan's reluctance to use the term 'assimilate' also. 'Ooh, nobody likes that word', I say.

'No, nobody likes that word in the International College. Hypothetically, they could spend anywhere from two or three weeks, up to a term or a semester in the International College, depending on how their English is improving, but depending also on their confidence and their social development. Then they come straight into class: students who've moved to Australia, been at the International College, living in the boarding house for a month or two and over they come, to Chiswick.'

I ask, 'Have you ever thought about what their previous musical experiences might be?'

'Yes, I ask them. A lot of them have instrumental experience ...'

'On Western instruments?', I interject.

'Yes. Many of them play piano, flute or violin and often they're very good at those instruments, which I believe is a result of lots of practice. Many of them are also quite good at reading from the staff. Their English skills are often very, very poor so they take a lot longer to pick up the things in class but we have a very supportive ESL programme available so we teachers can give our material to the ESL support staff to work through with the students.'

'And do you find that they participate fully in the classroom?', I ask.

'Yes, on the whole. There are some exceptions, but yeah, I think it's, they observe music as being as subject that they can have fun in but also that they can learn. A lot of them say "Oh, nobody has ever sat me down and taught me about what the interval between these two notes is, or what this rhythm is called, and why it makes the sounds that it does, or explicitly examined beat and rhythm and melody and chords." No one has ever taught that to them, so they come from a different musical experience entirely: one that I think is based on sitting down, learning pieces on your instrument and doing lots of practice and so that the musical learning is just sort of expected to come naturally out of the practice, which they have shown – to some degree – it does. With a little bit of guidance, however, it's a lot more successful.'

I ask, 'Have you had students talk to you about any non-Western musical experiences, the folk songs of their country? A student who's instrumental learning was based on non-Western instruments?'

'Last year we had a student who is now in Year 12, playing a Korean flute. A very interesting and ancient instrument on which she played a lot of what I would call folk-based melodies: legato, repeated, "singable" patterns. Her performance on this instrument was technically quite proficient and very communicative. There have been a couple of students who play native Korean instruments.'

I'm quite surprised to hear this – I suspect that this Year 12 student was Isabel, but I don't want to ask Sam at this point. Regardless of whether the performer was Isabel or not, I am surprised that she didn't mention this during our conversation about traditional Korean instruments. Perhaps she didn't know? Perhaps she had forgotten?

I continue my conversation with Sam. 'Do you think that repertoire is something you can include in your classroom?', I ask.

'I'd like to. I think by Grade 11 and 12, is when you start to look at music from all different cultures. I don't discriminate based on where a piece of music comes from, but if it's not a piece of music that's useful to me in terms of the musical stuff that it's made of, then it's probably less likely to find its way into my classroom. As much as I'd like to sing songs from all over the world and just have a good time, my kids aren't going to learn anything. So, I have to be specific about the repertoire that I choose. If a piece of music came my way, and it was, say, from Korea and it contained the five notes of the pentatonic scale and some basic rhythms then there is nothing that would stop me from using it in the classroom.'

'But the sequence that informs your teaching is drawn from a Western framework, therefore it's difficult for non-Western musics to fit in with that', I suggest.

'Yeah, for sure. There's potential, I think – I mean pentatony is quite prominent in Asian folk music. But I feel very strongly about the material that I need to teach and I wouldn't let anything get in the way of me teaching what I needed to teach, in terms of the sequencing of knowledge.'

A critical race theorist would have a field day with Sam's words here! Sam positions 'the sequence' as culturally neutral, as an arbitrary that justifies the exclusion or oversight of musics outside the Western tradition. I continue, 'Do you think students get the sense that some musics are more valued than others based on the repertoire that's used in the classroom?'

'I do think that, and I think that that's where I fail as a teacher to open up more, a wider range of material to my students.' Sam pauses to reflect on what he's just said.

'I think what I could do ...' He pauses again. 'I think our music does come from a variety of cultures. OK, maybe not cultures but from a variety of geographical locations. I need to know more about where the music has come from. I think the kids do actually really respond to that extra-musical information: where it's come from and what it meant to the people that were singing it, when they were singing it and why ... And I forget about that so often in my classroom, I just start singing and I just say "Here, learn another song, learn another song, learn another song."'

'Without putting it in context for them?', I ask.

'Exactly. And the students never ask because they've gotten into the routine of their teacher just teaching them new songs but I think, yeah, I would like to, I would really like to start to think about how I can engage them a bit more in the historical significance of the music that we sing because I think it's very important, we're performing music that's special, it's lasted the ages because it is special and they do have interesting stories to tell. So, yeah, that's probably something that I should consider more in my classroom and in that way make it more explicit to the students that they are learning music from a variety of different places.'

There is a contradiction in Sam's ideas emerging here. On one hand, 'the sequence' is positioned above all else, necessitating the use of repertoire that is drawn from particular (Western) traditions. By using a Western lens to measure a music's value, non-Western musics will never measure up (Koza, 2001). On the other hand, he recognises that he can do more to provide a broader range of musical experiences and contextualise those culturally and socially. I wonder if this about-face is because he is 'thinking/reflecting in action' throughout our interview, or if these are genuine tensions in his beliefs.

Leaving the field

Again, as I leave this case behind, I try to make sense of what I have seen and heard here.

Sam is a young teacher, and was essentially hired by Chiswick College because of his training in Kodály methodology. The philosophy adopted by the music programme at Chiswick one based on the belief that all students can participate in this activity. Based on singing, it attempts to mitigate some of the disparity in the students' musical backgrounds that would be highlighted if the students performed on their own instruments. The belief that all students can develop some level of musical understanding, knowledge and skill through the course of study provided is what underpins the classroom music programme that Sam and the other teachers deliver.

However, the design of the curriculum preserves Western art music as the reference point. Despite the school's resistance to the term 'assimilation', I observe little evidence of displacing dominant values by incorporating those of non-dominant groups, in the music programme or in the school more broadly. This is thoughtfully reflected upon by Isabel, a student who is eager to share with me her varied musical experiences although she doesn't feel confident enough to share them with her music teachers.

Sam's habitus seems to be closely aligned with the values of the school: deviating from 'the programme' doesn't appear to Sam as a viable pathway (see Bourdieu and Passeron, 1990), meaning that some of the ideas that Sam has expressed to me over the course of this project about ways that he might make music more meaningful to particular students remain untested in practice. I wonder if it is Sam's lack of experience or the historicised and institutionalised 'method' that is limiting Sam's ability to be more responsive to his students' needs and desires?

Towards the end of our research process, Sam begins to reflect on what he reads in this narrative, prompting him to ask questions of his practice that he hasn't considered before. He hasn't yet been able to answer those questions, but tells me that he continues to think about them. He has temporarily left

Chiswick College – his position has been held for him while he travels and teaches overseas. His story is one that is to be continued ...

Note

1 An abridged version of this narrative appears as 'Unpacking the habitus: Exploring a music teacher's values, beliefs and practices', *Research Studies in Music Education* 37(1), 93–106. doi: 10.1177/1321103X15589260

7   Jan Laws at Blackfield State High School

As I approach the school in my car, I am left with little doubt as to the central role of music at Blackfield State High School. Highly visible from the road, the Music Centre is an imposing structure, with large silver lettering labelling the building as such. In fact, as I discover later, this building also houses the hall – a space used for music, sport and general school gatherings. The building's signage, though, is clear – Blackfield State High School Music Centre.

Having learned from experience that everything takes longer than expected on my first visit, I have arrived a little early. As I sit in my car for a few minutes, waiting for my appointment time, I observe a large group of Blackfield students exiting the church grounds on the opposite side of the road and returning to the school campus. This strikes me as a little unusual, and I make a note to ask about the relationship between the school and this church.

As I enter the music centre for the first time it strikes me as a vibrant, busy, slightly chaotic place, with students constantly coming and going. In my first few minutes in the staffroom there is a steady stream of students knocking at the door – I soon discover that the first concert for the year is being held the following week and there is a music camp fast approaching (which all the music teachers will attend).

All of the music staff – the Head of Department, classroom and instrumental teachers – share a single staffroom. With the itinerant instrumental teachers sharing desks, there are sometimes more teachers than chairs to sit on, although the teachers are so busy that it is rare for them to actually be in the staffroom at the same time. All of the classroom and instrumental teachers take multiple ensembles, which rehearse before school, at lunchtime and after school.

Introducing Jan Laws

Jan is a teacher in her mid-fifties and was born in Atherton, a small town in far North Queensland. She has been teaching music and English for 33 years – in her position at Blackfield State High School for the past 18 years, and prior to this in a number of regional centres around the state. I ask Jan to tell me about her experiences of schooling.

'I lived in Atherton all of my school life. So I went to the Catholic primary school and then I went away to boarding school for a year (Year 8) and then I went back to the high school in Atherton for two years (Year 9 and 10). And then I went back up to boarding school for another two years (Year 11 and 12). I'd always played the piano. I started playing in Grade 2 and so I just, I don't know, I just stuck to it. But in those days there was no classroom music. So I just did AMEB (Australian Music Examinations Board) theory and piano.'

While I'm intrigued by this unprompted early insight into Jan's music education as a child, I prompt her to continue telling me about her upbringing in more broad terms. I ask, 'So you lived in North Queensland for all your schooling life?'

'Yes, and then I came down to Brisbane and went to teachers' college, did three years there. When I finished, I was placed in Townsville, where I was for two years. And then I got married and we moved to Rockhampton, I was there for four years. And then my husband got transferred to Brisbane, and I taught at Sunny Park State High for a year. And then we got transferred back to Atherton! Much to my dismay, because I thought I'd escaped! And we spent nine years there, but that was when I had my children, so I didn't work for five and a half years. Then I went back on to do a lot of contract and supply work around the area before I went back full-time. And I was there for three and a half years and then we got transferred, or my husband got transferred back down to Brisbane and so I have been here at Blackfield State High since 1993.'

Jan describes her heritage as Italian-Australian. 'Well, my parents are Italian. They were born in Italy, but I was born here. I learned to speak Italian when I was young. We always spoke English at home, because my mum was worried that it would disadvantage us at school. But my grandparents didn't speak English so I used to communicate with them in Italian. So I always understood everything. Recently I've been back to Italy – I spent three months in Italy in 2007 and then another two months last year and I went to a language school. So I'm fluent in Italian, which helps in choral music.'

Again, Jan's telling of her story returns to music. 'You mentioned before that you played piano through your childhood?'

'I started when I was in Grade 2. I went to a Catholic school, so I learned piano from the nuns all through primary school. When I was at the high school in Atherton I used to go to the convent for lessons, and then when I went to boarding school I learned from the nuns there. I loved piano, I never wanted to give it up. And I used to practise. I used to get up at, I don't know, six o'clock in the morning to practise for a couple of hours before I'd go to school, when I was at Atherton High School.'

I ask Jan what made her want to keep going with piano.

'I don't know, I really don't know. So many people start learning and they just get sick of it. I just never did. My sisters and brothers all learned as well, but they fell by the wayside. But wherever I was I kept going with it. I just always liked it. I don't know why.'

Blackfield State High School

'I don't have to be putting out bushfires'

During our first meeting, Jan gives me an introduction to what I can expect to see at Blackfield and why she enjoys working here.

'This is a good school. You'll find that out. A large number of students are in the instrumental/choral programme, and in my Year 8 classes, a third to half of the students in each class plays an instrument. It is great to just be able to do my job and not have to cope with behaviour problems.

'Our admin is very strict, so behaviour is really good. You won't see a kid out of uniform in this school. Each year for the last five years has gotten easier and easier because the kids are so cooperative. I don't have to cope with students throwing chairs and things like that, stopping other kids from learning. And so it's getting easier and easier to do your job. The admin work really hard to provide a learning environment where the kids can focus on their work, where there aren't all those distractions.

'The academic standard of the school has really improved in the last few years. In fact, we had eight OP1s (the highest ranking for tertiary entrance) last year and five of them were music students. This is the first time we have had so many. Normally we only get three, maybe five. We also have a French immersion programme that attracts gifted and talented students. The school numbers are capped, which means that anyone who doesn't live in the area can only get in on academic grounds or if they've done an audition for music or if they want to do French immersion. We're losing our tail end. We had no OP 24s or 25s last year (the lowest rankings).'

From what Jan has already described to me about the school's clientele, I am interested in hearing more about the school's enrolment policies. Getting an appointment with Barry, or 'The Boss' as the teachers refer to him, proves difficult. I make appointments with the receptionist but repeatedly something comes up at the last minute. When I arrive for my fourth attempt, he is available to speak with me, or he will be shortly. As I wait in the administration building, I note how similar the space is to those I've seen in other state high schools. The reception area contains mismatched furniture, dated linoleum on the floor, friendly but savvy reception staff, used to dealing with teenagers. From the moment I introduce myself to Barry (and receive no reciprocal introduction, leaving me uneasy about how to address him), I feel like I am taking up too much of his time.

I ask Barry to describe the values of Blackfield State High School for me.

'So it's a traditional school and our prime focus really is on academic excellence. And then we've developed music excellence. We have to take any student from within our catchment area, but our enrolment basis for non-catchment area students is based on the student's ability to contribute academically or culturally to the school, or both. So we've got those two programmes. As part of the academic excellence we've got French immersion programme. My line is always, well, you can go and join a football club, you can join a tennis club, you can join a music group, but you can't join a school outside of school hours. So our prime focus is on academia. And as a result of that I think a lot of the academic kids that we get into the school are music kids too, so the programme has grown because we're getting that quality of kid through that is multitalented.

'We believe the discipline within the school allows it to be a really good learning environment, that there's no disruption in classes. No behaviour issues. So the kids are focused on their learning.'

This is something I have noticed in my visits to the school – the emphasis on discipline is evident in the students' dress and grooming, in the way they interact with adults as they move about the school. I read a message on the daily student notices:

> A reminder that girls' hair is to be fastened in a single ponytail at the nape of the neck – no braids, no plaits, no loose hair around the face. A plain school ribbon should cover the elastic. Bobby pins should be used to secure any loose strands of hair.

Barry continues. 'It comes back to discipline or structure as being a major thing within any school learning environment. And I think it's a major thing in music, as you would know, to have a really good ensemble you've got to be very disciplined. And I think this aligns with the values of the broader school: "well, it's just what we do here", then the kids are disciplined within the ensembles.

'While it's a friendly environment, it's not whacking kids or anything like that, but it's a disciplined environment … We're on about excellence; we're striving for the best outcome. And I think no matter whether it's in music or whether it's in academia, we say to the kids "We want you to do the best."'

I wonder if this is a slip of the tongue, whether Barry really meant, 'do your best'.

Jan assures me that this is what Barry would have meant. 'He can be very abrupt at times, but his message to the kids is really about reaching their potential and doing the best that they can.'[1]

Families of Blackfield State High School

In my conversation with Barry, I ask Barry about the socio-economic demographic of the school's clientele. Barry suggests that I can look up the school's ICSEA (Index of Community Socio-Educational Advantage) rating myself on the federal government's MySchool website (Australian Curriculum Assessment and Reporting Authority, 2011).

'You'll see that we're probably just a little bit above average in terms of socio-economic backgrounds. And, I mean, we've got some very poor families in the school. We've got some very rich families. There's a spread. And also [a spread in] abilities. We don't have an SEU (Special Education Unit), as such, but we do have a Learning Support Unit. And we cater, probably there's about, we identify around about 20 students out of 300 [in each year level] that have significant learning difficulties.'

I ask why they don't have an SEU. 'Is that because students in the catchment area have another school that they could go to with an SEU?'

'No. We've just never had one and we've sort of never had the need for one here.'

'So are there individual students with physical impairments?', I ask.

'Well, we've got II [Intellectually Impaired] kids and we've got hearing-impaired kids. But we don't have physically impaired kids because of the nature of the buildings. You see the three-storey buildings here? We just couldn't cater for that.'

I wonder how Blackfield has avoided been taken to court by a tenacious parent of a physically impaired child – there is certainly precedent for this type of action.

The ethnic diversity of the student body was one of the first things I noticed on my visits to Blackfield – the enormous variety of skin colours (although I cringe as I write this – am I making a judgement about the level of diversity based on my observations of skin colour?), and the occasional hijab. I ask Barry to tell me about the religious and ethnic diversity and what that means for the school.

'There is a significant Christian population within the school. Who identify as that. It's always had a history of that.'

I'm somewhat surprised that this is where Barry begins. I ask if he thinks this is because of the school's location.

'Probably. If you have a look around you've got the Assembly of God Church over that way.' Barry indicates the direction as he continues to speak. 'You've got the Adventist Church here. You've got Baptist Church upon the top of the hill, which used to be run out of this school before they built the church up there. And I think it's [the school's] got a reputation, I suppose, as being a school for "good kids", if you know what I mean. And so that attracts more Christian type of people to the school.'

Christianity seems to be deeply embedded in the school's ethos – this is the first state school I have seen that begins their weekly 'parade' with a prayer led by the school chaplain. There are non-compulsory religion classes held a few times each term for students in Years 8, 9 and 10. (Jan tells me that this is why the students go to the church across the road, more for the reason of the school lacking a suitable venue than because of any association with the church.)

Barry continues. 'Having said that, we've got a significant Muslim population in the school. It really is multicultural.'

I say, 'I did notice that just looking around the school it does seem to be quite multicultural. Would you say there are possibly families where the parents don't speak English at home?'

'Sure there are', Barry replies. 'We pay interpreters if we have a parent interview with people who don't speak the language. When we've had parents who have been profoundly deaf, we've had signing people in the school for parent–teacher interviews. I suppose, the only time it becomes a significant issue if a kid is in trouble and you've got to communicate with the parents who don't speak English. And there's a barrier there. And that's why we get interpreters in because the kids obviously [when they need to act as translators] hide the situation from the parents and tell them different stories.'

There are some difficult questions that come to my mind, questions I'm uncomfortable asking: is there any communication with parents apart from when the student is in trouble? Is this only for NESB (Non-English Speaking Background) families or for everyone? How do the school's culture and values extend outside the school boundaries and into families if you don't communicate with them? Is there a disjuncture between school and home values in some cases? How are students affected by that?

Music at Blackfield

Barry continues, describing the development of the music programme in the 21 years he has been principal at Blackfield.

'The music programme is a significant programme. It adds significantly to the tone of the school. When I came here we had a C-grade concert band and about half a dozen string kids I suppose.

'I'm an ex-music teacher. So we grew the programme over the years. It adds to the tone of the school ... for two reasons. One is the quality of the students you get into the programme and secondly the, you know, I guess the tone of the school in terms of showing excellence.'

It is becoming more clear the longer I spend at Blackfield just how serious Barry is about attracting 'quality students' and 'showing excellence', and how these values are embedded across the school. When Barry says 'we grew the programme', the 'we' he is referring to includes himself, Jan and the Head of Creative Arts – although, as Jan says, 'we were the ones doing the work. He was really supportive, but it was us doing it. Except for the school musical production – he directed that every year.'

Barry continues. 'Now, you can see that we've got four concert bands, so there are different levels of players in those, we're providing opportunities for players of different abilities. And four string orchestras.'

I wonder, however, about the level of diversity that having four concert bands and four string orchestras encourages – is there a place for the guitar player, the Irish fiddler, the pop musician?

When Jan reads this she feels the need to clarify: 'It's not just string orchestras and concert bands. I mean, that's what the instrumental teachers are expected to run as part of their job, but we've got so many more ensembles than that. An orchestra, a Celtic string group, two percussion ensembles, three jazz bands, a jazz combo, a brass band, plus the four choirs. We [the teachers] make a choice to provide those options.'

'That's a diverse skill set that the teachers have', I say.

'It's more that we all really want to do it. Those of us who teach in the classroom get a couple of extra spares to compensate for the time we spend in rehearsals – I have rehearsal before school four mornings per week.

'We also have a guitar teacher and a singing teacher who come to the school. The parents have to pay for those lessons, but they still have the opportunity to learn at school.'

Jan describes differences in the programme now compared with when she first started teaching at Blackfield.

'When I started at Blackfield in 1993 and I was taking the choir I was frustrated because I didn't really know what I was doing.'

I ask if this was Jan's first experience with choral conducting, when she started at Blackfield.

'No, I had had choirs before, but nothing too serious. It was just get a group of kids together to sing for speech night. It wasn't a real choir. But here at Blackfield, the principal wanted a *good* choir and a *good* instrumental programme – he said, "I want a programme that rivals Ridgepoint" (a neighbouring state high school with a long history of excellence in the arts). So he gave us extra spares (free periods) to build up the programme … The first choir that I had [at Blackfield] was made up of all the students from Years 9–12 who did music as a subject. It was compulsory for them to be in the choir. I found that absolutely abominable, because nothing works if people are forced to be in it. So the very next year, when I found out that kids were not taking music as a subject because they didn't want to be in the choir, I made it optional.

'I don't want to have to cope with kids who don't want to be here. Barry's very competitive and wanted us to enter competitions, too. I could hear that my choir was not very good compared to the others. It was very frustrating; and that's when I decided I just had to do something to improve my skills. I started going to a lot of the ANCA (Australian National Choral Association) activities because there were a lot of good conductors there. In 2000 I enrolled in the Master of Music Studies, majoring in choral conducting.'

'Everyone can sing, they just need to be taught'

I ask Jan about the structure of the school's extensive choral programme. She describes the make-up of the four choirs, three of which she conducts herself. Chorale is the school's premiere choral ensemble, an SATB choir for students in Years 9–12. Jan also conducts Cantabile, for Year 8 girls, and Canticum, the Years 9–12 girls' choir (some of these girls also sing in Chorale). There is a Male Chorus for boys in Years 8–10, taken Jan's colleague, Greg.

The only one of these choirs that is selective is the Chorale. Jan explains, 'Everyone can sing, they just need to be taught.'

'So any girl who wants to can be in Cantabile or Canticum?', I ask.

'Yeah. I do audition them, but I take pretty much everyone. I don't do the auditions for the Year 8s, because they come in from their primary schools at the end of Year 7 to do the instrumental audition and it's just too much time if they come down to me as well … So the instrumental teachers do the auditions – just to see if they can sing in tune and to decide if they're alto or soprano.'

In a Cantabile rehearsal, a girl sitting near me, Evie, is one of the few in the group who isn't singing in tune. Jan gives the general area that Evie is sitting in quite a lot of attention during the rehearsal – she sings their part in Evie's direction, seemingly in the hope that she will catch on. At one point, Jan approaches Evie and holds a finger to her own lips: 'Shhhhh'.

Several months later I ask Jan how Evie is going in Cantabile.

'Poor old Evie. I love Evie. She's the most gorgeous kid. She's my most enthusiastic member. She's in the French immersion class, very bright little girl. Always wanted to sing. Devastated that nobody would ever have her in the choir in primary school and was quite ecstatic when she got put into the choir here. And for some reason …', Jan pauses. 'You see, she can sing in tune by herself, so obviously when she did the audition she must have just been asked to sing a song and could sing it and so was put in.

'And for some reason she got put in the alto section, which was a big mistake. So at music camp I had Amanda (one of the other music teachers) working with her and we decided to see if she would be better in the soprano section where all she had to cope with was singing the melodic line. And she's just done beautifully. Because that was really … I used to have to walk over and say "Evie, can you just listen?" You see, she doesn't have a very good ear. I teach her, I have her for classroom music, and she wasn't very good at the aural sort of tasks that we've done in class. So yeah, she doesn't have a good ear, so she's not pitch matching very well. So we've put her in the soprano section and that seems to have solved the problem.'

I express to Jan my relief that Evie isn't going to become one of the people who spend their life believing that they can't sing because of what a music teacher told them as a child.

'That's exactly right! And particularly since she was such a keen little girl. And I just think it's awful that they've been told in primary school they can't sing, because I just think that shows a lack of the teacher's ability to deal with them, because everybody can sing. I know that obviously there is an incredibly small percentage of people who are literally tone deaf, but I think they are exceedingly few and far between. I would say I probably only ever come across two in my whole teaching career, which has been more than 30 years. So everybody can be taught to sing. You just have to find the right place for them or maybe give them a bit of extra help. If they want to do it, they'll get there.'

Music for all? Year 8 music at Blackfield

I ask Jan which year level she likes teaching the most.

'I love teaching the Year 9s and 10s because they have chosen music as their elective and are therefore eager to learn. Also, the class sizes are smaller, so I find it a bit easier to give the students the individual time that they need.

'I don't really *love* teaching Year 8. Because it's compulsory, there are so many kids who have decided from primary school that they don't like music; fewer now than a few years ago, though. It's really hard when they come from the primary school with preconceived ideas. Also, if they had wanted to do music they would have done it by now. I was a great believer in this "music for all" idea. When I started going to the [Kodály] Summer School, I really thought, "Music for everyone – this is right!" But then I got back to the reality of it and I'm like, there are some kids who simply are not interested.'

'And the other thing is that we only have the Year 8 classes once a week. So it's really hard to get any continuity. By the time they come back to you in a week, they've been to maths and science and phys-ed, etc. and they've been here, there and everywhere. Do they remember what they did last week?'

As I observe a Year 8 lesson, the sense of discipline that Barry described to me is evident in Jan's routine with this class, much more so than with the lessons with the older students that I have observed. The students enter, move to their set seating position and remain standing in front of their chair until there are greeted and invited to sit down. There is a sense that these students need to be managed more carefully than the Senior students. Despite the formal routine, and the fact that she has told me she prefers teaching the older students, Jan's manner with the students is friendly and encouraging.

Jan tells the students that they are going to be working on the keyboards for the next part of the lesson. The students already have a page of three-note exercises that they are learning to play. This is part of their assessment and is something the students have been working on all year. I am somewhat amazed that, within a minute of being told to move from their desks, all of the students are seated at the keyboards and have begun work. The classroom is organised in a way that facilitates fast, smooth movement from desks to the keyboards and computers, but the students are so engaged and eager to complete the work that there is no time wasted getting started. Students share the keyboards – each is set up with two pairs of headphones – although most appear to be working independently of their partner, with very little conversation between the pairs of students.

Jan provides the students with a variety of levels of difficulty that they may work at – more experienced students are encouraged to take the more difficult options, although all students are given the opportunity to try.

Jan instructs the students to come to her at the piano at the front of the room when they think they are ready to be tested. Immediately there is a line of students eager to show what they have done. Jan hears each student, offering specific positive feedback as well as suggesting areas for improvement. A very advanced piano player gets plenty of praise for an excellent performance, but also more musically sophisticated feedback and more complex tasks to work on.

I am enlisted to listen to the students' performances while Jan deals with an unexpected problem with the power supply to the keyboards. (Jan laughs when she reads my description of 'unexpected problem'. 'It happens all the time', she says.)

The students remain at the keyboards practising for around 20 minutes of their 70-minute lesson. Towards the end of their practice time some students become less productive, spending time experimenting with changing the sounds on the keyboard while their partner plays. However, there are still more students coming to the front of the room to perform for the teacher and the students working individually continue to work on the exercises that have been set.

In some ways, I wonder what Jan is talking about when she describes the Year 8s as difficult to teach – to me, they seem lovely, compliant, engaged, and enthusiastic about participating and learning in music. At the time that the previous conversations took place it was still early in the year; Jan had only had these Year 8 classes for a handful of lessons.

'None of that really applied to the classes you observed. Those Year 8 classes were some of the best I've ever had. Both were specialist classes – one was the French immersion class, and the other class was a TIC (Technology Integrated Curriculum) class – and they have to be very strong academically to get into those programmes. But usually the Year 8 classes are a bit more difficult than the elective classes in Years 9–12.

'I wasn't as successful at that [creating a music programme that engages all students] as I would have liked to be. I'd love to think that all the kids in Year 8 were just really enthused about music and that I was getting to every one of them. But I don't feel that that is the case. I don't think I've been 100 per cent successful in that.

'I think if they wanted to do music, they would have done it before in primary school. And so it makes it difficult … It comes back to the problem where you do have the kids who've done a lot of music and the kids who have just had bad experiences with it and don't want to do it. And you have them in a class together.'

'That's something you've mentioned a few times – that if they really wanted to do music, they would have started before Year 8', I say.

I relay a story to Jan based on a conversation I had with James.

'[Year 8 music] it just got that initial passion of music started. At first, I didn't have a guitar. Well, sort of had a guitar. It was like this old piece of junk that my uncle used to play when he was like 14 or something. And like, when we were kids we just pretty much battered it. It's got all drawings on it and we smashed it … so it's got holes in it and it had like five strings, no maybe four. I don't know. And so I had that at home and I was just trying to figure stuff out. Then when I came to school and we started doing the guitar unit, like D-chord, G-chord and stuff. And from there I just kind of like, wanted to play the guitar. I went on the Internet and I got tabs and I did all this stuff. I really wanted to play guitar, so I did it and I just\consistently kept doing that a bit. [I'm] not very good, but, like, I can do enough to be happy with what I do.'

'So he's one of the ones who probably could have had the opportunity of learning in primary school but for some reason didn't', Jan says.

I suggest to Jan that maybe there are others like James, who missed out on an opportunity. 'Your main feeder schools all have instrumental programmes, but some children would come from other schools, some will come from other states. Some may not have had the opportunity to learn an instrument because of their family situation, because of financial reasons.'

'Well, that's probably true. Some might not have had an opportunity because the instrumental programmes in the primary schools can only take a limited number of students, so they test the kids. And I guess parents wouldn't necessarily go out and get private lessons if they didn't get into the school programme, although most families in this area could probably afford to, if they thought it was important. They might not learn an instrument because they didn't like it at primary school – one of the feeder schools has a music teacher who lots of the kids say they don't like.

'So our Year 8 course is designed the way that it is, as a big revision of the basic literacy skills so that we can have everybody at least on the same page. And give everybody the opportunity of taking it in Year 9 if they want to.'

When Jan reads this again the following year, she adds to what she said previously.

'The current Year 9 classes really prove that – we have three Year 9 classes this year (around 70 students; approximately 25% of the Year 9 cohort). And there are lots of students who haven't learned an instrument before, aren't in ensembles. They'll probably never get an A, but they'll manage.'

'Musicianship, of course, is always central to everything'

Jan's teaching emphasises the development of aural musicianship and music literacy skills. I ask Jan to elaborate on what she thinks is important for the students to learn.

'I mentioned listening to different styles of music, but underlying all that is not only identifying the various styles of music but also being able to analyse and identify the musical elements in that music; to be able to identify the instruments they hear, to be able to work out the ostinato rhythm, etc. Musicianship, of course, is always central to everything.'

This value system underlies the programme at Blackfield, although the four classroom teachers approach their teaching in different ways. 'We all have to do the same test paper. So basically [each teacher] teaches it in their own way, whatever best suits them. And that's the best that you can really do, I think. When I started using Kodály methodology, I provided everyone with lesson plans for Year 8s – I still write lesson plans for myself. It didn't really work though, because we are all experienced teachers, and everyone has their own way of teaching. I could follow my lesson plans but the others didn't really want to follow them. It's too difficult for someone else to tell you OK, now you're going to go into the classroom and you're going to do this, this and this. It just doesn't really work.

'We've got Sony Acid (a software package that uses pre-recorded loops) now and Greg's going to use that with some of his classes. And I think that's fine but ...', Jan pauses briefly. 'I think it's a bit like making a packet cake – it tastes fine, but it doesn't get you any closer to understanding how to make one for real. A loop-based composition could sound really effective, but there's a limit to what you can do with it.

'I think if we were offering a different sort of course, if we were offering a more technology-based course it might be different. But we still believe that musicians should read and write music, whereas other schools don't. Greg's just been to a seminar at another private school where all of the kids are really actively engaged with computers and they actually learn guitar and they work at their own pace on guitar. And they have apparently huge amounts of students doing music in Year 12. But their push is not to put out kids who can actually read, who are musically literate. Whereas we don't, it's not our ethos here. We believe the kids should be able to read and write music.'

'So they are actually learning some literacy skills even if they haven't read music before?', I clarify.

'Well, we try to teach them some literacy skills. Whether they learn them or not ...', Jan's voice trails off.

'However, [in Year 10] we do have a "Setting up a Band" course for students who aren't as musically literate, and it focuses on pop repertoire.'

I ask her what is involved in that course.

'Well, they actually learn how to run a band – it's called "Setting up a Band" and that's exactly what they do. They form bands. So they all have to learn to play or sing something.'

I ask, 'And can they learn an instrument as they go in that course, or are they expected to have some musical experience?'

'Yes, they can. It makes it a lot easier, obviously, if they have already learned music. But essentially, Greg shows them what to do on the bass guitar, for example, so they can do that. Or they learn to play a rock beat on the drum kit. The second semester is song writing and it is also very pop-based.

'But getting back to the core classroom subject. I think the students should develop their aural skills, gain an appreciation and understanding of many different styles of music, the confidence to perform in these styles, the ability to create music that expresses style and the ability to identify the way the musical elements have been used.'

I ask Jan about how approaches teaching musicianship in a way that allows all of the students to develop at their own level.

'[When we work as a whole class] I do scaffold the activities, as I said before. For example, if I've set them a memorisation task, I set out the steps. For example, the first step is to memorise the first three bars. Once you do that then you move on to the next. If you can do the whole lot then you do the whole lot. So there's always that inbuilt scaling, I think in pretty well all of the activities that I give them.'

I clarify, 'So you're trying to give a scaffold to those students who might be a little bit weaker or less experienced, so that they can do something and they can come back to you and say I memorised the first three bars and feel happy about that. That they experience some success and they feel that whatever they can do, as long as they put some effort in it's OK?'

'That's exactly right. I think it's pretty easy really. Music lends itself to scaffolding. Like, for example, today with the Year 9s we were working on a piece called "Rhythmic Rondo". It's in compound duple time, that's something we've been working on. So the first step is clapping one line at a time. The next step is to do both. The next step was then to swap hands, so do the bottom part with their right hand. So there's always, inbuilt steps ... So whenever I set homework or set activities I'll always give them basic step, next step, next step.'

I see evidence of this scaffolding in action during a melodic dictation exercise with Jan's Year 12 class. Jan begins, jokingly referring to the students' attempts at dictation in the previous lesson. 'Because you all did so badly on the last dictation, I'm going to give you the rhythm for this one.'

One of the brighter students asks, 'Couldn't you not give us the rhythm so that we can learn?'

Jan replies, 'I know that some of you can do it without the rhythm but ... How about, if you want the rhythm, come up here and I'll give it to you. But the dictation's not very long, maybe you'd like to try without.' Some students take advantage of this offer for help, while others choose to go it alone.

When we discuss this later, Jan explains why she took this approach. 'Some of them just really struggle with dictation. For some, not having the rhythm wasn't going to help them learn – they need the help and if they don't have it they just get frustrated. And now that aural skills isn't assessed in the new syllabus, we don't spend as much time practising dictation in class. I've always found that some kids can just do dictation – they just have a good memory. Others really need to practise if they're going to improve.'

Repertoire selection

At the time that I am observing Jan's lessons, the Year 12 class is studying art music exclusively in their class work. I know that some of the students perform in more contemporary styles for their performance tasks and the music making that they participate in outside of the classroom. I ask Jan to tell me about what informs her choices when it comes to repertoire.

'Well, it's decided by the units in the work programme. The focus in the Year 12 unit that you saw is to get them to understand the differences between the different periods (Baroque, Classical, Romantic and Twentieth Century). So there's strong push to understand the orchestra and development of the instruments in those times so that they understand why a piece sounds classical. Instead of just saying it sounds classical, they can say well it is classical because ... So that's the focus in that unit.

'But it's not always based on art music. Year 9s start with a world music unit. Then they do a unit of musicals and then rock music. And then the Year 10s do Australian music and jazz in first semester. And then they do art music in second semester, basically to give them some knowledge to take into Year 11. Year 11 starts with a foundation year, so we do a folk music in first semester. And that's when you go over all the basics again. So if you do have kids who haven't done music in Year 9 or 10, for example, maybe they've been playing in ensembles – maybe they're quite advanced instrumentally or vocally but they haven't done the subject – there's still a lot that they've missed out on. So the folk music unit is really good for that, for analysing structure of songs and things like that. And then in Year 11, second semester is a whole semester on rock music, actually. So the art music is limited to one semester in Year 10 and then first semester in Year 12 – second semester Year 12 is a musical and then they do their own thing – they choose their own project for fourth term. So basically, you know, we try to give them a wide range.'

This programme is quite similar to what I studied when I was at secondary school. One of the implications of structuring the units by style means that there are periods of time (a whole term or semester) where the repertoire studied may fall outside the preferences and strengths of some students. I'm interested to know whether this is the case for some members of Jan's class, and I have a good opportunity to find out with the students Jan has nominated for me to interview. Ben and James eagerly agree to an interview as part of my study. Both are remarkably articulate young men ('the main reason that I chose them', Jan tells me) and are eager to talk to me about their experiences of music and to know more about my project. Both are avid music makers outside of the classroom, but there are differences in their musical backgrounds.

Ben began playing viola when he was in Year 3, which he has continued to learn through the school group lesson programme. He plays in the school orchestra and string ensemble, in addition to singing in the school Chorale, which Jan conducts. His school subject choices are English, two maths subjects, chemistry, Japanese and music. Ben is interested in pursuing a degree in engineering at university the following year. I ask Ben to tell me about why he takes classroom music.

'Well, I originally chose physics in Year 11, but I decided I didn't like it as much as I like music. Music is usually the highlight of my day, because I can be silly in it.'

I laugh. 'Do you think that affects the amount of work that gets done?', I ask.

'Yeah, probably.' Ben laughs. 'I don't know, I think because we only have three assessments per semester and it's always towards the end of the semester we can get away with a bit more mucking around.'

I ask Ben if that's the only reason he takes classroom music, as a break from the demands of his other subjects.

'I just like learning about music theory pretty much. There really aren't any styles that I don't like listening to and analysing. I am always analysing songs thinking, "OK, that does that there ..."'

'You mean the songs that you listen to in your own time?', I ask.

'Yeah, the songs that I'm listening to, and that builds the skills for analysis, which I think helps. I write a lot of dance, electronic songs as a composer. There is this thing called "chip music", and it's basically using games systems and old computers for the soundchip qualities of the analogue soundchips. I have a program on my GameBoy which I use to write music.'

I've never even heard of this before. 'So explain chip music to me?', I ask.

'It's not a genre, which people don't realise; it's just a way of creating the music. So a lot of people make dance, house, trance music using the GameBoy because it has a really nice de-tuned synth sound.

'Because I can learn from what other composers have done and I can apply it to my own work. Essentially, I think, everyone is a product of what they hear, I think if you didn't listen to other influences you'd have nothing to go on. That's generally what I want to get out of classroom music.

'For me music is a way of being rather than something I study. Because you listen to the radio and you hear that person's done this, this and this and you can hear, and kind of melodic dictate what they've done. Whereas people who are, say a classically trained piano player, their teacher says "Here's a piece of music" – they don't think about it in that way at all. They don't really see past the sheet. Which I think is part of being a musician.'

While the types of music that Ben listens to outside of the classroom aren't really included in the repertoire Jan selects, he has found a way to connect the classroom learning experiences with his own music making. James, on the other hand, has found it more difficult to make that connection. In my conversation with James, he lists an enormous range of composers, performers, genres and styles that he has listened to at various points, including J.S. Bach, Jimi Hendrix, John Coltrane and Kings of Leon. James identifies himself as a singer and a guitarist, who only started learning guitar in Year 8, because of the opportunities provided in the classroom programme (see vignette earlier in this chapter). I ask James how he finds the unit the class is studying at the moment, given that the Programme Music genre is outside of his musical preferences.

'For performance, generally we can choose what we want, and that's good for me. But for composing and analysing it's pretty difficult for me, because I'm not from a big musical background. Like a music theory background. I can pick things up quite easily. I'm good at maths, I'm good at science. And like, I get concepts. But because I've never had an upbringing that included reading music, [I find] it's really hard analysing stuff. I'm really shocking at sight reading – anything with a score, I'm pretty rotten at doing all that kind of stuff.'

I observed the class completing an analysis task through score reading and listening to the recording. I ask James how he felt about completing that task.

'I can kind of read rhythm … Like I could kind of follow it, but I still like, if you were to ask me what chord everyone was playing and blah, blah, blah, it would take me like ten minutes to sit down and go A, G … no, F … OK. So, I'd be horrible.'

I ask how he copes with the assessment tasks, particularly the analysis essay.

'I'm [a] very flowery [writer]. I'm good at English. So most of the time, because I grasp the concepts and I have an OK ear, so I might think, like "It's driving" (rhythmically). I don't know if it's syncopated or not. But, whatever, cool. If it's driving it should be syncopated, so I'm going to write that anyway. So it's half guesses, half, like, using big words and making yourself look as though you really get what you're talking about.'

'And how does that work out for you? Does that convince your teacher that you know what you're talking about?', I ask.

'Not very well. It used to. I probably get about a B or a C. I don't expect myself to be doing any better than that, even though I do better in performance and in my other subjects.

'Like now, we're doing classical music or programmatic music. I'm a bit worried because I don't, like … I'm going to get on with the composition and somehow figure out how to write it, an orchestral or like a string quartet or something like that. Like a piece that's classical. And so that's a bit scary for someone who's only well versed in pop music. It's also partly because I'm a bit lazy.'

I ask, 'do you see the point of doing the analysis and composition? Do you see how that learning might connect with the other music that you do?'

'Yes, I see the point but sometimes I just feel like … too little, too late, almost.'

'That you don't have the skills to understand?'

'Yeah.'

James is a high-achieving student, even if he tends to rely on his natural ability rather than good study habits. He is passionate about music and is eager to learn and understand different styles, but his lack of formal music education outside the classroom has limited the level of success he experiences in classroom music.

Student motivation: 'It needs to come from them'

Jan frequently refers to the need for the students to be motivated if they are to be successful in music.

'So, if they're motivated then they'll move on, they'll progress. If they're not motivated, well, you know, I do my best to try to motivate them. But ultimately I think it needs to come from them.'

'Do you think that they start to develop some motivation seeing that other people actually went home and practised that and they can do it?', I ask.

'Yes, definitely. Because I still remember in the early days … I still remember one particular girl who decided that she wasn't going to participate – she didn't like to sing. But then she saw that everybody else in the class was doing what I'd set for homework and she was the only one who hadn't done it. Pretty soon she was doing it too. That's the sort of kid that she was; she was very good musically. I think she thought it wasn't cool, so why should she do this? When she saw everybody else was getting into the spirit of it, she was fine with it then.

'I have found, though, that the problem with kids who haven't done a lot of music before is that they aren't as motivated as those who have. And so I do find it a little bit difficult to find suitable material. I think because they are not prepared to put as much effort into it as they need to, because for them to come up to the same standard as some of the others they need to put in extra effort, it just sort of doesn't really happen for them. Music is a hard discipline; it doesn't happen by accident. You have to work hard at it.'

I ask if Jan ever finds students who are really motivated to work but maybe don't have the background, just because they haven't had the opportunity for that before.

'There are those. I have a girl in my Year 12 class who's very, very musical. I can see that. She does a lot of song writing and performing, but because she doesn't have the same theoretical training that the others do, she always feels that she's a step behind. She came crying to me one day, because I had set them a canon to memorise. It was a difficult one because I was trying to push some of the more talented students. But because I hadn't scaffolded it for them, she was having difficulty. We discussed ways of going about it and told her that if she could do four bars I'd be happy. So that's the way that it went.'

'And was she able to do those four bars?', I ask.

'Yes, she's been trying. She's been trying, because she's a really good kid. Gradually she had the whole canon memorised. Actually, she's got a great writing style; she's really good at English. I love her analytical responses, because she always uses such great vocab to describe the elements. Sometimes she doesn't quite hear things properly; she doesn't always identify the correct instruments. But she writes a good essay.

'We don't get many kids who aren't very musically inclined [choosing to study Music in Years 9–12]. They simply don't choose the core subject (see discussion below of "Setting Up a Band") because they know how good our music kids are and they realise that they are going to be at a disadvantage, I think, if they go into a class where they know someone's really, really advanced.'

Jan's comment's here align very closely with the academic environment created by the school – one where academic achievement and competition are encouraged. The marking system in Queensland schools doesn't actually allow for students to be graded comparatively, yet the students learn to position their achievements in relation to other students' achievements.

'There's such a strong focus on academic excellence and achievement here that some students who are very bright but maybe don't have a lot of musical experience feel like they won't achieve at as high a level as they might want to. I had a student a few years ago who was very capable, very bright, but she wasn't going to top the class. And she knew that if she took biology she could.'

On the first day of my observations, I see evidence of just how motivated the students in Jan's classes are. As we walk to the classroom, Jan conveys her concern to me about the amount of teaching I will have the chance to observe. 'Well, to start with, the Year 9s are doing NAPLAN practice, which I should have told you about, so you won't see their lesson. And the Year 10s will just be doing prac, so I won't really be teaching them much.'

I assure her she need not worry, that these things are just part of school life. I begin to wonder what Jan means about not teaching the students because they're doing prac – she doesn't strike me as being a likely 'hands-off' teacher when the students are rehearsing.

Jan confirms this when she reads this later: 'I can't believe I said that – "won't be teaching them", of course I'll be teaching them! It just won't be a formal lesson, because they'll be in different rooms and I'll be going around to the groups.'

The students are given around 45 minutes of the lesson to rehearse for their small-group performance assessment. On our way to the lesson, Jan had described her approach to 'doing prac' with the students. 'I used to, when I first started teaching, give the students almost no time at all because they just wasted it. I still don't give them a lot, because I don't want them to feel like they have time to waste.' Jan puts a number of measures in place to discourage the students from wasting time – no group is allowed to move to a rehearsal space until they've told Jan the names of their group members and the piece they're performing.

This period of movement is chaotic – the students are anxious to get started, so rush to give Jan the details that she wants. Some students don't have a piece to play yet and need access to the school's music collection. Others need to print lyrics, chords and tablature from the Internet. The ensembles and the genres of music represented within the class are diverse – some sing pop songs with piano or guitar and drums, some play orchestral instruments that they learn outside the classroom. Some play their own choice of music, some play or sing pieces chosen by their private teacher and others ask for Jan's help in choosing.

It is clear that the students enjoy these sessions – they are eager to begin and some seem worried about wasting their limited time. I overhear one group, who are hurriedly trying to print out the lyrics and chords that they need to start work on their song: 'We need to go back and jam, we don't have a lot of time for this.'

Two boys fail to move when the rest of the class does. 'What are you two doing?', Jan asks them. One of the boys replies, 'We don't know.' 'Well, you were supposed to have decided by today.' When Jan leaves the room to look for music for another student, the boys walk over to a keyboard and sit down. To my surprise, they take the page of canons with them and begin playing fragments of the canons that they were singing as a class. They quickly diverge into riffs and motifs from other songs that they know. After a few minutes Google appears on their computer screen: thoughts of the performance task are forgotten for now.

Jan returns to the room, having found music for the students who needed it. She asks the boys what they are doing. The boys still don't have an answer for her. Jan quizzes them briefly on what instruments they each play: both play trumpet (although one says he 'doesn't play anymore', he has a trumpet and can play it). Jan leaves them for a few minutes, while the boys stand idly beside her desk, not talking to each other, as if waiting for something to happen.

The first group of students head back to the computer again, printing chords for a different song this time. All of the group members are clearly bothered that this is taking so long. One boy calls, 'You print the chords – we'll meet you back in there' as he heads back to their practice room. The boy left at the computer says to himself, 'Why is everyone in such a hurry?'

When Jan returns to the classroom the trumpeters are still waiting beside her desk. She hands the boys some books of duets for trumpet. The boys sit down at their desks and pore over the music. A few minutes later, the boys have made their choice. They move back to the keyboard (neither has his trumpet here today). The boys struggle to play the part on the keyboard, so they decide to put the notes into Sibelius so that they can hear what the piece will sound like.

I decide to take a tour around the other classroom and rehearsal studios. In one classroom, a group of girls is singing a song that they know without accompaniment or lyrics – correcting each other when needed. One girl reminds her peers of the need to sing this song with an Australian accent if they're going to do it 'right'.

In a small studio, a string trio independently practise their parts rather than trying to put the piece together straight away.

The bell rings. Some students move to pack up, others stay into their lunch-time to keep rehearsing. Jan stays a few minutes longer, offering advice to students who haven't finalised their choices yet, reminding some of the less prepared students to practise their part before next lesson.

I am surprised not only at the level of focus that the students show towards their work but how widespread it is across the class. I ask Jan why she thinks this is.

Jan pauses, a puzzled look on her face, as if looking for the words to answer my question that is, to her, completely obvious: 'Because they enjoy it.'

I challenge her to elaborate on this: 'I've seen lots of students in other schools who enjoy really enjoy prac but are much less focused, much less goal-oriented perhaps?'

'Look, I think it's probably got to do with the whole ethos of the school. Most of these kids in Year 10 are in the ensemble programme, and most of them are very keen to do well at music. And most of them are performing at a reasonably high level. A lot of them are probably considering taking it on into Year 11 and 12, and further. Two of the students in that class go to the

Young Con (a programme for high school students run out of the Queensland Conservatorium). So I just think they've been turned on to music basically and via the various methods, various ensembles that we have. Because we don't only have the instrumental ensembles, we have the choral work as well. So just the whole package, I think. It's not just the classroom music. I think it's the combination of the instrumental and choral programme with the classroom music that these kids have just become so motivated and just love music so much.

'But also they love working with their friends as well. I try and encourage them to work in groups where people are of the same standard as they are, or maybe from a similar sort of ensemble. And so I think that's better. But they do love working with their peers.

'Well, that's the other thing, too. As long as they're working on a piece that they really like then they will get motivated and work really hard at it as well. But if you don't find the right piece for them, then they do tend to get a little bit disillusioned, I guess.'

'Do you get involved in the process of helping them choose?', I ask.

'Oh yeah, they have to choose. Well, I give them several options. We've got lots of music here so I say look you can do this, you can do that, you can do the other. You can choose something of your own, but I have to approve it. So they have to bring it to me and tell me what it is that they want to do. As long as I think it's a suitable standard and appropriate for the unit, then that's fine.'

'Do you give them suggestions or if they're having trouble?', I ask. 'Like, "this song would be really good for your group?"'

'That's right. And try to pick the appropriate level stuff as well. Because that's the important thing, it's got to be achievable. If you give them something that they think is totally out of their reach, well you're wasting your time. But that's the good thing about prac because it's just got the inbuilt levels in it so the kids can perform at whatever level they're at and perform well. It doesn't matter if one piece is an AMus (Associate of Music diploma awarded by the Australian Music Examinations Board (AMEB)) standard piece and another one would probably be Grade 1. It doesn't matter. It's how they perform it, not what they perform. So that's a good way of catering for individual differences.

'Also, they're all very motivated and quite competitive as well, because they want to get in there and do well. Conscientious is the word I was looking for. There are a lot of really conscientious students in there and, for them, less than an "A" is not good enough.'

The sense of academic competitiveness that I noticed at Chiswick College is evident here as well – the students measure their achievement against each other, not just against the criteria and standards. This seems to be facilitated, almost encouraged, by Barry and by Jan.

I ask Jan about what role she hopes music will play in the lives of her students after they leave school. 'What do you hope the students take with them from classroom music when they leave school? Only a small number will pursue tertiary pathways in music, what would you like the others to get out of Year 12 music? What role would you like music to play in their post-schooling lives?'

'I hope that when students leave they have a well-developed ear for music and an appreciation of lots of different styles; popular music for those "art music snobs" we have and art music for the more popular-inclined. I would hope that they continue their musical pursuits in community groups – choirs, bands, orchestras, etc.'

Outside the music department: Year 10 English

At one point in my visit to Blackfield I have the opportunity to observe one of Jan's English lessons. Jan has always taught at least one English class in her time at Blackfield, and this is her preference. The other music teachers also teach at least one other subject.

We venture across the school to Jan's English classroom. As Jan greets the students as they enter the classroom, Jan asks the students to correct their uniform. This is the first time I've seen a student with their shirt out, or their socks not worn correctly. The lesson begins with a quick spelling test – words from the list for Year 10 contained in the workbook that all the Year 10 English classes use. The correct spellings are given, and students are instructed to write out the words they misspelled three times each. This is followed by five to ten minutes of journal writing, and then a continuation of the task that was started in the previous lesson – reading aloud from a play script to be studied this term.

I ask Jan about the structure of the lesson. 'Is starting with a spelling test something that all the teachers would do?'

'Look, that's probably just me, because I'm a bit old-fashioned in terms of literacy again. I'm passionate about literacy in music and I'm passionate about literacy in language as well. We've always had a very strong emphasis on literacy here, and grammar. But the spelling thing, to be honest, I use that as a settling down, focusing activity. I do believe that kids do work better in a structured environment. I start off with the spelling and then they do their journal entry. But that usually only takes the first five or ten minutes. It settles them down and then we can get onto whatever else that we're doing. What I care about is they're writing something and everybody is writing a paragraph each lesson. Because you know how hard it is to write essays. While they're doing their journal entries I will often talk to them about things like topic sentences and supporting sentences, in the hope that it might wash over into when they're actually writing an essay, that they'll think about that structure. Even if they don't find it particularly easy, at least they will have the confidence to get in there and write, because that's the first step. I mean some of them still say I don't know what to write, so often I will give them topics, suggestions of what they could write about. Such an old-fashioned approach to English …

'And I still remember a conversation I had with one teacher – I was teaching Year 9 English at the time and she took the same class over when they went into Year 10. They were really quite a noisy class. And then one day she decided to give them spellings and she couldn't believe that the whole class went quiet. She'd never had that before. But it was because, she said to me, it's because I had trained them because I won't have talking in spellings. We have silent time. We write. We correct. We write out. Nobody talks during spelling time. So these kids, you know, it was like Pavlov's dogs. They were trained not to talk during spellings and they fell back into that habit.'

Jan interacts quite informally with the students despite the very formal routine of the lesson. Her teaching style differs remarkably from what I saw in her music lessons.

'The class just isn't like my music classes – like you saw, in music, I can set them a group task and they'll work hard at it because they like it and they like making music with their friends. In English, they get off-track all the time – they're not as motivated. So the routine helps to get the lesson started.'

The underlying belief that Jan has about the need to settle the students down and get them working quietly aligns well with the whole-school approach to discipline and work habits.

Leaving the field

The culture of strict discipline and academic excellence underpinned by an expectation of a certain level of conformity and homogeneity is how I would characterise Blackfield State High School.

Barry, the school's principal, has built this culture deliberately. As Jan says, 'The school culture is part of the reason parents send their kids here – it's what they want for their kids.' If I view my observations through a lens of Noddings's (2005) ethic of care, Blackfield is doing its job – it's providing an education that meets the needs of their clientele in a generalised way. I'm uncomfortable with some aspects of what I see at Blackfield: I don't see what having a 'conservative' hairstyle has to do with learning, nor do I particularly like the inclusion of Christian rituals in a state-funded, multi-faith school.

But it works for them. According to the most recent parent opinion survey, 92 per cent of parents who responded were happy with the school and the quality of their child's education. Blackfield has a waiting list of students from outside the immediate catchment area who wish to attend. The classroom music programme is oversubscribed; with enrolments in the Year 9 classes being closed when the three classes are full. All of the music classes I observed were filled with students who are engaged with music for the time that they learn it. There are so many students wanting to be in choirs that they need to continually create new groups because they grow too large for the rehearsal space. All of the classroom and instrumental teachers take as many ensembles as they can possibly squeeze into their timetable, because they want to provide as wide a range of performance opportunities for the students as they can.

Jan's classroom is orderly and well managed, with students who are compliant and appear eager to learn. There are some very musically experienced students who look for ways to challenge themselves, while there are others who are less experienced and struggle a little.

However, I wonder about the students who are missing from the music classroom. As Jan said, and as I observed when I visited her English class, the students who take music aren't a representative cross-section of the school's clientele. I wonder about the possible reasons for this: is it because the musical styles valued by the classroom programme are more attractive to particular types of students? Or could it be, as Jan believes, that students who don't learn an instrument feel that they are unlikely to measure up against those that do?

Note

1 In the months that passed between period of the fieldwork and the member checking, Barry had retired. Email communication was attempted but no response was received. Barry approved the transcript and consented to its use here but was unavailable for comment on the interim research text.

8   Jayden Wood at Seaview State High School

Prologue

I sit in the office of one of my colleagues at the university, bemoaning the fact that I am yet to find a final research participant for my study and my PhD clock is ticking. The delays I have experienced in the approval process with Education Queensland (see p. 40) have cast doubt on whether I would be able to complete my fieldwork in time. I had contacted several school principals by email (no reply) and phone (never available), and was starting to feel that I would never find a teacher and school to fit the criteria I needed to round out my set of case studies. Julie asks me who I am looking for – I describe a female teacher, not a beginning teacher, in a state school, preferably in a low socio-economic area. 'I know someone – I've never used her as a research participant before, I'd been saving her for a really good project. And I'm sure she'll say yes. Actually, she's coming next week to do a guest lecture for me.' Julie suggests that I should stop by her office after Jayden's lecture so that she can introduce us.

As soon as I see Jayden I recognise her immediately – the two of us had attended high school together for Years 11 and 12 (I had completed my junior high school years elsewhere). I didn't recognise her name because she uses her married name, she didn't recognise mine for the same reason. Despite that fact that our career choices have been remarkably similar, we haven't crossed paths since leaving school. As we chat over a cup of tea in the staffroom, Jayden asks me about my research project (Julie has already told her that I'm looking for a participant). As I describe my study, I don't even need to ask her to participate – she's already agreeing to do so. I don't hesitate to accept her offer to participate and to take my proposal to her principal.

I feel an enormous sense of relief – the first sign that my fieldwork and dissertation will eventually get finished.

My first glimpse of the light at the end of the tunnel.

Introducing Jayden Wood

Jayden Wood is a 30-year-old teacher of 11 years' experience, all of which she has spent at Seaview State High School. Jayden doesn't have much time during the school day for an interview – her timetable is too full. In addition to her classroom duties, Jayden has the responsibility of organising the school awards ceremony. She also lectures for a course in music curriculum one evening each week and works as a marking assistant for other lecturers. After a long email exchange trying to set up a time, we agree to meet on a Monday evening at her home. As we sit at her dining-room table, Jayden's inquisitive two-year-old daughter comes in and out of the room while we talk.

I start by asking Jayden to tell me about her experiences of music at high school.

'Really?', she says, referring to our shared experience of high school music. I had forgotten until the moment that I asked the question about this close association. I hadn't thought about how this would influence the interview.

We both laugh. 'Pretend I wasn't there', I say.

'OK. I remember going to Grade 8 music and it was the first time I'd realised that a lot of students weren't really good at music. It was quite funny. I'd just been a bit sheltered until then. It was at a lower level to what I was working at, because I'd been doing outside piano exams and flute exams. So when it came to Grade 8 music it was very, very easy. There were students in there who couldn't read a treble clef – it was as though they hadn't done primary music at all and I was in the same class with those students. I was thinking, "How is this not easy to you?" I actually remember thinking to myself, I hope Grade 9 music is not like this, because I would just be so bored. Then from Grade 9 onwards it got a lot more complex and a lot more challenging. It was really, really enjoyable. So from there I loved it. I had a really, really good classroom music teacher who probably, subconsciously, has influenced me along the way. I mean, when I was at school I never wanted to do music teaching, I never really thought about it. And even talking to other teachers and preservice teachers about what they're seeing out there, I go "Wow, we were actually really lucky we had a really good teacher." So my experience was all positive. Even though there were times when I didn't do as well as I wanted to do in a particular area, I never actually found it to be a negative. It was actually empowering, and the teacher really wanted to help me to do better.'

This music classroom and teacher that Jayden refers to are the very ones that began to trouble my thinking around the purposes of music education. When I think back now, I can see that my position in the music classroom was one of privilege – I had access to knowledge and skills that other students did not because I learned music outside of the classroom, and I was able to draw upon that knowledge to achieve success. During a Year 12 music lesson, I remember thinking that I could just 'do it' – it had nothing to do with any teaching or learning that had happened in that class, only that I had, at that time, been learning music outside the classroom programme for nine years. There were others in that class who couldn't 'do it'. I distinctly remember thinking that, in the two years that we had been together as a class, nothing had changed – the students who could, still could; the others who couldn't, still couldn't. As I reflect on this now, I recognise that the hierarchy of 'haves' and 'have nots' (Koza, 2001) was maintained. Nothing had really changed. Our teacher was lovely – caring, engaging and knowledgeable – and I think she really tried to help everyone, but she was working with a syllabus that required more knowledge and skills than could be taught in a five-year programme.

There are tensions between our perceptions of classroom music education. Jayden's pedagogy is inspired by her own desires and preferences as a learner, and she views her students as wanting the same things she did from classroom music. When Jayden and I discuss my views of myself as a privileged class member, she doesn't want to put herself in the same category, despite the fact that we both had the benefit of experiences of music learning from outside the classroom.

I ask Jayden what how she feels reading my reflections on the same classroom events. 'I had a really different perspective on, essentially, the same teaching and learning events. I was wondering what you thought about that?', I ask. 'Did it feel like we were talking about different classrooms? Are you happy to accept that we just saw it in different ways?'

'I think so …', Jayden pauses. 'I found personally that there were a lot of things that I got out of classroom music that was very new and exciting, because I didn't do any other music activities outside of school, like the QYO (Queensland Youth Orchestra) or Young Conservatorium. So for me I can see how your perspective was very different – because you did all that stuff, maybe you were getting that stimulation from those activities.'

The school that Jayden and I attended was a private school, one with a busy and thriving music programme. Most of the students involved were in multiple performing ensembles (I was in five, Jayden was in six), which meant that there really wasn't time to take on commitments outside of school as well. Because I had only started at the school in Year 11, I was already doing those things, and I wasn't prepared to give them up (which caused tension at times when performances and rehearsals clashed). Jayden explains to me that she feels that she missed out on something because her teachers (for piano, flute and classroom music, as well as ensemble directors) didn't pass on information about these opportunities.

'I started there in Year 8 and I felt that it was very insular, that we weren't really encouraged to do anything outside of school, we weren't even really told about what the options were. So I guess that influences what I do with my students – I make sure that they know about what's on offer, after that it's up to them whether they take advantage of those opportunities.

'I think back to some of the resources that we didn't use so well – we had that computer lab in the classroom next door that we never really used. I think using all of the resources that are available is something that I always really try to do; I often put myself in very uncomfortable situations to try and learn new things. That means that sometimes I'll look like a bit of a dag in front of the class for the first few lessons, but I think it's for their benefit that I try those things.

'So, I'm not saying that everything at high school was fantastic, but for me, the big thing was the repertoire, and the content and history, and composing – those aspects I really enjoyed.'

What is evident throughout these conversations is that Jayden's perception of her own experience of music in high school is a powerful informant of her current practice, in the way she replicates the aspects that she enjoyed and remediates the things that she wasn't happy with.

Jayden continues to tell me about her tertiary music and education studies.

'After high school, I went straight to university – I did Bachelor of Music in Performance. I actually enrolled in the education degree to start with, but I changed out and went to just a straight performance degree. I think I always knew I didn't want to do performing, but I just really enjoyed music, so I thought it'd be good place to start, and then work out where to go from there.

'Then I did my Bachelor of Education externally and online, it was two years full-time and it was fantastic, a really good course. While I was doing my education degree I was teaching instrumental music and taking ensembles at Seaview and at the local primary school. When I finished my degree, I started doing a mix of instrumental in classroom. And that worked out really well.'

I ask Jayden what influenced her decision to pursue classroom teaching rather than instrumental.

'The instrumental teaching job was the one that was offered to me. I was still studying my education degree (externally), but I didn't need a degree to teach instrumental. It changed gradually, moving from instrumental teaching into classroom, each year taking on a few more classes. The reason for that is the mental challenge – I actually really enjoyed the complexity of teaching classroom music far more than instrumental. I was teaching Years 5–12, and I did get tired of teaching the basics. My strength I think is as a high school teacher, I didn't enjoy teaching the primary students. I was happy to do both at the start, but I figured out over the years that classroom teaching was what I really wanted to do.'

The school context

Seaview State High School is situated in diverse socio-economic area, with some expensive waterfront estates surrounded by what are traditionally working-class suburbs. 'It's a really mixed area', Jayden describes. 'There are some expensive houses around here, and we have students who come from there. There's a real mix. When I started here 11 years ago, the school was probably a bit lower socio-economically, but it's really built up in that time.'

As Jayden says this I am reminded of the similar situation at Blackfield, another school with thriving programmes in music and languages, also on the move upwards socio-economically, the mean demographic of the school pulling away from the mean demographic of the area.

'It is really diverse. I see students that come here whose parents struggle to buy school uniforms, and then there's parents who go out and buy their child a $3,000 instrument, just because they can.'

On the first day that I am scheduled to observe Jayden's lessons, I arrive at Seaview State High School a little later than I would like, but again, I have no trouble finding my way to where I need to go – a large complex, highly visible from the road, clearly signed as 'Performing Arts Centre'. The school is made up of a maze of two-storey brick buildings, all quite similar looking, with a few newer buildings mixed in. The Performing Arts Centre is one of these, containing classrooms, computer labs, performance and rehearsal spaces, studios for private tuition and practice, and a staffroom for the large performing arts staff. As I write this, I realise that Seaview is the only one of my research sites to have a performing arts staffroom rather than a music staffroom. I wonder about what this says about music education in schools (a discussion for another place) and how a whole-arts approach might be seen at Seaview.

On my third visit to Seaview I have an appointment to meet with Peter Barker, the school's principal. He is running a few minutes late, so I sit and wait in the reception area. When Peter appears, he greets me with a friendly smile and a handshake, accompanied by a profuse apology for keeping me waiting. I check my watch – it's a little less than ten minutes past our agreed meeting time. I assure him that it's no problem; that I've waited far longer for principals before. 'But you shouldn't have had to wait at all, I'm so sorry.'

After we enter his office and get settled, I begin by asking about him to describe the school's values.

'We've got a mixed population of students. We've got some that are amongst the brightest in the state, we've got some that are intellectually impaired. So we have a full spectrum of kids: in terms of athletic ability it's the same, in terms of creative arts ability it's the same. The important areas for us in this school, we've got a very clear articulated philosophy and objectives, which you would have seen. We specialise in creative arts, and we specialise in a sport development programme for football, soccer. And we've got a very strong science faculty as well.

'We take everybody from our local area and we probably attract a quarter of our population from outside our feeder area. They come for specialist programmes: they come for the arts, they come for soccer, they come for science, those sorts of things. We don't have any policies that we exclude anybody from outside the area, but it may be they have to wait for a place. We've got some things that are so popular that we can't fit any more students in, so they might have to wait for a bit. Our numbers are limited in some of the sport programmes and also some of the vocational things, like construction. It's unsafe to have more than, say, 15 students in a construction class. So, if we're full you might have to wait. And construction and those things are a new area that's really very, very popular.'

'It seems like Seaview has got a lot of VET (Vocational Education and Training) offerings across the school', I comment.

'We've got a good mixture, yes. Because we've got a full range of students we've got a nice balance. We maintain probably more subjects that count towards an OP than any other school in the area, significant numbers of OP subjects, and the VET certificate courses as well. There are schools nearby where only 40 per cent of students are OP eligible. So we've got probably two-thirds of our students are OP eligible and about one third aren't. But those students can get up to Certificate III in some areas, so that when they exit they can either go on to further study or be employed. The aim is a hundred per cent of them can do that.'

'Do you usually come close to that?', I ask.

'We do. We come close to a hundred per cent. The survey data from last year's Year 12s isn't out yet, but it's always interesting to look at that and see where there might be gaps and what can be done.'

Peter continues to describe the diversity of the school's clientele.

'Also, at any one point in time we have 50 fee-paying international students here. So we're recognised as an international school, we're accredited as an international school. And since I've been here, apart from the fee-paying international students, the mix of the population has changed. So when I first came here in 1990 it was pretty much a monoculture. But when you wander around, look around the school now you find an amazing, eclectic mix of backgrounds.

'Having some Chinese students come was an impetus to start Mandarin and now we've got the students who are not the international students who are now starting to learn Mandarin as well. And I work across the local primary schools as well. In one school, we're going to be offering Mandarin to Prep and Year 1 students and their parents shortly. And then we're going to offer it to Year 5, 6 and 7 across the area. So then as time goes on then we'll actually offer Mandarin as a second language in all the primary schools. So we'll build our language base, because I actually think that every single child needs to have two languages.'

'And how does having those international students here affect the curriculum or the way of working within the school?', I ask.

'It might affect some of the teaching, because it actually improves the teachers' skills because they've got to think about how they cater for the needs of those different students. So we have to do a fair bit of professional development to help them. We offer ESL support for them, of course, some of them. Some of the students speak English very, very well, particularly the ones that come from Germany or Italy or Brazil. They generally speak two languages, or even three, and do them all very well. But there is a need for the teachers to focus on pedagogy so they look at their teaching and learning more acutely. And we have to support them with that. Some of them struggle but they're getting better at it.'

As well as the excellence programme in languages, Seaview has a longstanding reputation within the community for being a music excellence school. I ask, 'How do you see the role of music and the arts in the life of the school?'

'Music is the soul of the school. If we didn't have music it'd be pointless coming to work. One of the great things is that Matthew East, our Head of Creative Arts, does a great job. He has a great knack for offering programmes and catering for kids who might not succeed elsewhere – because they're individuals, or because they buck authority, or because of whatever. But we have programmes and teachers that manage to cater for all of them. So we have students who go into symphony orchestras. We'll have students who go into jazz. We'll have students who go into rock or various other bands. So it's an amazing range of music. But also they do a great job with music industry skills (a VET course) so that students can learn about lighting and sound and stage. It just opens up the range of professions that students, either full-time or part-time, can be involved in. So the important thing for us about music is that any student can find a home there if they want to, in some fashion. So we have the ones who come through that we've worked with in the primary school who are already exceptional, and the ones who start here in Year 8 and find their niche and develop when they come here. So for us, the important thing there is it's for everybody, it's not just for the ones that come into the school as talented musicians.

'So for me, having a big and a vibrant creative arts faculty is important, but it's also important to be a community-based faculty. So part of Matt's role has been turning that Performing Arts Complex into a community precinct. You may have seen that it's full of other people all of the time. Yesterday morning there would have been a drama group in for the performing arts space. And you would see any time of the day or night just about anybody from the local arts community using the centre and working with our kids and those sorts of things. So what's important for me is that community interaction and community use, where the community can benefit and we can benefit because our kids get people coming in that work with them; artists, visual artists and performing artists coming in all of the time.'

'That's quite different to what I've seen in some other schools', I say.

'It was a vision Matt and I had. So it was our vision that everything that's here is a community thing. Especially the arts, which is … it's not something that you do in abstract. So for me, the important thing was that the arts aren't separate from art in life and community and those sorts of things. So you can make a living out of the arts or you can have a job and still have arts as well.'

The cohesive vision that Seaview has in their excellence programmes, particularly in music and languages, is evident across all levels of the school staff, from senior administration down to the teachers who implement the programmes.

Music at Seaview: letting the kids find their niche

As Peter has mentioned several times during our interview, Matthew East is the driving force behind the arts at Seaview. In his position of non-teaching Head of Creative Arts, Matt is responsible for arts curriculum, extra-curricular programmes and works closely with the administration team on matters of strategic direction in the arts.

'I guess I'm lucky that I can be so involved with the administration team, that my role is strategic. I've already got the timetable for next year.' (It's June when we meet; the following school year will start in late January.) 'I'm already working on it and I can ensure that the kids can do their English and maths and then have the rest of their programme as creative arts – there's kids that want to be able to do that. And I know the sort of possible scenarios of what they might want to do. Music kids are more likely to do a language. So I make sure that French or Japanese is never on the same line as music. A lot of my music kids will do drama, so there are a lot of clashes that I look out for.'

On my first day at Seaview I have the opportunity to sit in on an Arts Faculty meeting, led by Matt. He begins the meeting by describing the events planned for Senior Citizens' Week – he has applied for and been awarded a small grant to cover the costs of transporting some of the smaller performance ensembles to nearby retirement villages to perform. He continues on to matters of curriculum reform – the introduction of the Australian Curriculum (the content of which, at the time, is largely unknown) and the restructuring of secondary schools to encompass Years 7–12 instead of commencing with Year 8 which has provided a catalyst for reorganising the arts curriculum at Seaview. As Matt raises this topic, he indicates that he doesn't want to 'open up a can of worms', but that this is something that the teachers need to begin thinking about.

Later, he discusses this meeting with me.

'At the moment, Year 8s only do music and visual art – they do two periods of each every week. Now when the Australian Curriculum comes in, while we don't know what's going to be in it yet, we do know that students will need to do all the arts up until Year 8.[1] Now next year that might simply be two periods of music and two periods of art. But eventually when I change the whole thinking of my staff, and it will be a drawn out process but I will do it, it will be much more of a tasting plate so, as dance and drama are in there as well. It is very, very difficult to change the mindset of certain staff.' At this point, Matt asks me to stop recording. He describes the level of ownership that some of his staff feel towards their subject area, and the conflicts that are likely to arise as time is taken away from some subjects in order to include all the arts strands in the Year 8 programme.

Having worked at Seaview for 21 years, Matt has a unique perspective on the history of music at Seaview. I ask him to describe the underlying values of the music programme.

'When I arrived at the school there were 45 kids involved in music, in total. Sorry, not just music – drama and visual art as well. That was the arts in Seaview High School. So very, very small. There's about 300 now, a bit over. I built up the music programme very quickly just by simply making it interesting. I quickly established that there was a huge need for streaming: to provide both your board, your QSA music and a certificate-type course. We were the first school in the state to actually offer a certificate course in the music industry ... it just meant that the kids that just really wanted to sit there and strum guitar, or play rock music, didn't want to study anything serious with music, weren't really anticipating going on to be a music teacher or in the serious – I say serious, in a formal, I should say – music genre. They had their niche and they loved it. I remember at one stage that my class, every boy in the class and two of the girls, had all been suspended at some stage in that term. But they came to school for music, because they loved my class. A lot of those kids in the certificate courses, if you had them in the music class it would bring down the whole music class because they just don't have the interest in the formal music programme.'

Matthew's use of the word 'streaming' immediately sets off the 'equity alarm' in my head. I ask, 'When you say streaming, are the students restricted from changing from one course to another at any point?'

'Absolutely not. They find their own niche because we've had a lot of students over the years that have started in music and, you know, they haven't done particularly well. So we have a little chat and say "Maybe you would prefer to do music industry where you can learn how to set up PAs, learn to do recording, learn about copyright, work as a band. That type of thing." Then they give it a try and they do really well.'

I ask, 'Do you find students moving in the other direction? From the certificate courses into academic music?'

'No, they're usually the ones who will start off by doing both, wanting to do both. We do a fair bit of canvassing so the kids know what the difference is in Year 8 ... We make sure that we spend a fair bit of time, from about August onwards, coming up to when the kids are doing their subject selections, we let them know what the difference is with the subjects, with the specialist teachers going in and talking to the kids.'

This attention to providing the students information about the various options and supporting them in making the most appropriate choices is an administrative undertaking, something that is facilitated by the strong support from the administrative team, from Peter and from Matt.

Jayden's values and beliefs about music education

The wide variety of pathways on offer for the students at Seaview mean the music staff are numerous and diverse in their skill sets. Jayden primarily teaches the academic music offerings, what she calls 'core music' courses.

Lifelong learning

I ask Jayden to describe to me what she thinks are the crucial knowledge and skills for the students to develop in her classroom.

'Fundamentally, one of my goals really is to make them, and it sounds very clichéd, but lifelong learners. I know that most of them aren't considering music as a career path: I don't push them into pursuing a musical career or doing auditions for uni or anything. Every year there's only a handful, a very small number, who want to do that. I think the others take it because they just really like it and they see it as a part of a broader education rather than a career pathway.

'So I think it's important to give them the skills so that when I'm not around they can keep continuing and learning music without me. I honestly feel that it's important to give the students the right skills to be able to move forward when you're not there, to give them the tools to know how to use their music beyond Year 12. To me a successful student can leave Year 12 and have options, know what they want to do and how to go about it, and feel confident.

'When I'm teaching a concept to the class – it could be how to do an assignment, I'm not just teaching them how to succeed in that particular assignment but giving them the skills so they can transfer them to other areas. So if they came across another assignment at one point they've got that skill set there. So a lot of my teaching is very much underpinned by that. I kind of find it refreshing that they don't need me all the time. They can go away and they know how to research. And that can be applicable to any task that I give them then. They're not given a new assignment and sitting there saying "Well, how do I do it?"'

'How do you view your role in that process?', I ask.

'I really want to teach them the right technique, because when they go home and I'm not there to look over their shoulder, then they're not playing the keyboard with one finger and they should be able to try to play harder songs. So by setting them up with the right hand position, they should be able to find a song that uses the same notes and play it successfully.

'I do the same thing with guitar. I spend the first few lessons on naming all the parts of the guitar and actually working out how to read chord charts. We spend a lot of time on that. Then we start with two or three easy chords and we all sit there together and I just check every single student.

'I'm very big on being flexible and encouraging and letting them work at their own pace, but I do a little bit at the start to get them all on the same page. I definitely don't go "We're learning guitar and keyboard kids, off you go!"

'I also think that it's important to allow the students to try and perform on an instrument that they might actually enjoy and engage with. A lot of the students have never touched an instrument apart from recorder. I'm very much adamant that they learn the correct technique – so for keyboard, the correct hand position, actually reading the music and learning what the notes are. What they find is a real sense of achievement, especially for those students who've had such a bad experience of music in primary school. That they can actually play music successfully in high school.

'They do have to work towards prac assessment, but we don't do prac in first term with the Year 8s. There are some classes that I have refused to do prac with, but for the most part I find it's a really good bartering tool. I say to the students, "Well, if you can't get this theory work done in the first part of the lesson there will just be no prac today." And that usually works really well.

'I use different techniques to get them to experience success really quickly. One method I use is to get the students into three groups and play something simple like "Wild Thing". I'll give each group one note or chord and then point to each group and they'll play their note, or they close their eyes and listen. They can hear that they're creating a song. Within the first lesson they're saying, "Wow – I was part of making music." It's that kind of spark that I find creates a bit of a snowball effect; they want to keep going because they think that they'll be able to do it well. I've had a lot of students who never played keyboard before, have then done keyboard in class and by half-way through the year their parents have gone out and bought them a keyboard because they're just so keen to do it at home.

'There is one boy who is going onto YouTube, as there's a guy who posts videos on how to learn the piano. So he's been watching and learning visually from these YouTube videos. To me that's not ideal, obviously, because I come from a classical piano background.'

Jayden's comments here perhaps point to her beliefs about instrument learning as drawn from the practice of Western art music. Her background as a classically trained pianist explains her emphasis on having good technique, or the 'right technique', as Jayden describes it. Within the practice of Western art music, the pedagogical model of the master–apprentice lesson is so entrenched that it is assumed to be the most effective way to master an instrument (Jørgensen, 2000; Lehmann *et al.*, 2007), and this is reflected in Jayden's reluctance to accept this boy's approach as an alternative.

Jayden continues. 'But that's still a success, because he's engaged. He was one of the students that I had to have an interview with his mum at the start of the year because he was failing. And his mother said she just didn't know what to do with him. And then she said "Oh yeah, he had private piano lessons a long time ago" – he's never even said to me that he'd had lessons.

'I don't mind how he's doing it, but then I'll have to go and correct his technique. The only thing is … I think there's problems down the track when those students go on to Year 9 and 10, 11, 12, are they limiting themselves by learning things on YouTube and not developing the right technique, not learning to read? Unless I can see and monitor the technique of the guy on YouTube, and whether he does have good technique for the students to copy from, I don't think it's ideal.'

In the senior classes, less time is devoted to individual or group practice, and more to developing composition skills and content knowledge – historical and analytical information about the musical styles and genres covered in the unit.

The Year 12 students are completing a unit entitled 'Innovators', which appears to be focused on working through twentieth-century art music styles.

The new style for today is neoclassicism. Jayden begins by putting up a slide with the key features of the style, and talks to this slide for a time, making reference to previous styles studied. The students answer questions and contribute to the discussion, but their responses tend to be limited to recall of content from prior lessons.

The following slide says:

> You have been given a piece of classical music and asked to arrange it in a neoclassical style. How will you manipulate the music to make it sound twentieth century?

I wait for the music to be played or a score distributed, and it seems that some of the students are waiting as well. No music is produced. The students begin to discuss the question with their friends and compile a list of techniques that could be used. After a few minutes of discussion, these responses are then shared with the rest of the class.

I ask Jayden about this later. She comments, 'But why do you have to put your music first? What I was trying to encourage with this activity is abstract thinking, to get them to experiment.'

'It certainly is abstract, but I didn't see them experimenting – this was a discussion activity.' What Jayden seems to be suggesting is that she doesn't want the students to feel restricted by the ideas of other composers. I ask Jayden to elaborate and clarify.

'I think my point was that I don't want to give them all the answers. What I wanted them to do was to think for themselves, to construct the knowledge for themselves, to discuss and have a conversation about how a composer might make something sound neoclassical. Then, the next lesson, when you weren't there, I played them some examples of neoclassical works. But I wanted them to come up with the ideas first.'

The lesson continues. By way of transition, Jayden plays the students a piece that they have studied earlier in the unit. 'What was this piece called?' Students begin call out their guesses, none of which are correct. Jayden provides some prompts: 'The one with the graphic score, with the violins, that you all loved?' This goes on for a few more minutes, while the recording continues to play. A student asks, 'Do you actually know, Miss?' 'Yes, I know, of course I know!' Jayden replies. 'Then tell us!' The piece is eventually revealed as 'Threnody to the Victims of Hiroshima' by Penderecki. Jayden seems appalled that none of the students could remember the name of the piece that they had listened to previously.

The lesson moves on to a composition activity: in groups, the students are to take a simple melody and arrange it using neoclassical techniques. After sitting for an hour, the students are eager to move and begin work on the practical task. Jayden retreats to her desk, which is positioned at the side of the room, where it provides an ample view of the classroom. Most of the students begin discussing the task immediately – with the exception of two students. One girl approaches Jayden at her desk and begins chatting, before demonstrating her newly written song, singing and playing guitar. This soon attracts a small group of students around Jayden's desk. I wonder if they gather to listen to their classmate or if they are waiting to seek advice from their teacher regarding the work that has been set.

After the allocated time has passed, Jayden calls the group back together. 'I know you've had a huge amount of time to create this masterpiece …', Jayden says, her voice dripping with sarcasm, 'but let's hear them.'

The first group performs 'Mary Had a Little Lamb' in major seconds, another group presents a 'remix' of another nursery rhyme with a drum track from the keyboard. Some of the groups seem to be interpreting neoclassicism as remixing. The bell has already rung, but they run a few minutes over time to hear the final group's performance.

Jayden's desire for her students to be lifelong learners is perhaps drawn from her own passion for learning. She refers to her desire to 'keep up to date' with technology, she engages in leadership roles that she thinks will be challenging, she takes on teacher education work at a university, even though there is barely enough time in the day (or night) to fit it all in. However, it's hard for me to see the evidence of how this philosophy informs her pedagogical choices.

Year 8: an opportunity to re-engage

As Matt and Jayden have described to me, Seaview has multiple strands of music classes in all year levels. In Year 8, they have an extension class. I ask Jayden to tell me how that works.

'I don't actually teach that subject, but it is the advanced instrumental students from the feeder schools in the area … for students who want to pursue music at a more of an advanced level. As you would have seen when you came, there's students from my (core) Year 8 classes who at the end of the term still can't tell me what a treble clef is.

'So to be fair, they put a Year 8 music extension class together. There's normally anywhere between 40 to 60 students – it's quite a big class – with two teachers assigned to it, and every week they have to have ensemble rehearsal in their class time. That's to extend their performance skills. And they also have composition, theory, audiation, those kinds of things as well. I have personally never taught that stream, but it's worked really well, because a lot of the students then flow on to the Year 9 popular music [course] or the Year 9 core music that I teach. And it's very flexible – there are students who go into the extension class and say, "This is too hard, I can't do it", they can then go across to another Year 8 class that is more at their level.

'I've had a few students come out of the Year 8 extension class into my class and have done very well. And there are other students who just lose interest, they don't want to play their instrument anymore, and they can't be in the extension class if they're not going to play in the band.

'To me, there's not enough students going on with music in Year 9. There are always two classes – one core class and one popular music class – and they tend to be quite full, overflowing. This year, the majority of the students in my Year 9 class, the core class, have come from regular Year 8 classes rather than the Year 8 extension class. Some of the students in the extension class decide just to continue with band, with their instrumental lessons, and some decide to drop their instrument as well.

'And we often have a few students who drop music in Year 9 when they have a problem with subject choices, and come back in Year 10 or Year 11 – too many subjects that they want to do, or a clash in the timetable.'

'What do you see as the purpose of the Year 8 core programme?', I ask.

'For me, the biggest problem is that I have a large majority of Year 8s who come to me are completely disengaged from music. They may have had a really bad experience of music in primary school. And I often just have that conversation with them – with all my Year 8 classes in their first lesson I actually ask about what their experience was and actually listen. It's quite interesting. I have students who tell me that all they have done for the last three years in music is sing Beyoncé songs, or that they haven't touched instruments, or "No, we haven't done theory."

'It's about having to unify them all together, so that they're on a common ground with their knowledge, and then to give them an experience of music that they might actually connect with and find engaging.

'Using Year 8 as a medium to re-engage them in music as much as we can, get them all to a common ground, give them enough skills so that they have the confidence to go "Well, I can do this." It's a very slow, gradual process of building them to a point where they can enjoy music class.

'I had one very, very challenging class last year that, by the end of term 1, the entire class apart from three students were failing. And they just said, "We hate music, we're not interested, we don't care" – that's what I was coming up against every lesson. So here was me trying to find repertoire, thinking what can I do … But by the end of the year, I had all the class – except for a handful – that were actually passing. I managed to turn them around and, slowly but surely, change their attitude. And actually a couple of those boys in that class are taking the Year 9 popular music class this year. I really thought I'd have none.

'It's a year that I think involves a lot of nurturing, finding what they like and enjoy, and it's really building their confidence. It's a very difficult process to get through to the end of the year.'

'Do you think, for the most part, that you have some success with it, as far as turning them around?', I ask.

'Definitely. And I know a lot of them aren't going to take music in Year 9. To me success is that they (a) pass the subject; (b) find it enjoyable; and (c) that they can sit in class and discuss the music that we're listening to intellectually. I really try and encourage them to appreciate and accept music, and if they don't like something, "That's fantastic, let's talk about why you don't like it." I think there's a problem in some primary schools with how the kids are treated, with how their thoughts are treated. I say to my students, "I like to hear what you have to say." I think some of them are a bit shocked that I'm willing to listen to them. So I'm really getting an idea of where they're coming from.'

'It's like making a kid eat their veggies': you may not like it, but it's good for you

Repeatedly throughout our interviews and conversations Jayden refers to the importance of choosing the right repertoire that will engage students in music learning. I ask her to explain what factors influence her choice of repertoire.

'I think there are probably a few things that influence my choices. First, I kind of select my repertoire on what I think they need to know. Sometimes it's not the most engaging repertoire for them. I know they mightn't connect with it, but it's really good for them to learn. It's a bit like making a kid eat their veggies – they need to do this.

'I normally have a discussion with the students in the first lesson about what styles of music they usually listen to and what they want to cover in class, because they have a bit of ownership over what we cover. Ninety per cent of the time they say that they want to cover what they know and what they like. Some of them would be quite happy to do heavy metal for 12 weeks.'

I ask Jayden how she decides what specific pieces to include with a particular class or year level.

'I look at the clientele that I have and seeing what styles they're into, and trying to expose them to things that I think they would never ever listen to. Looking at my class and thinking, "How can I shock them?" at times. That's probably what drives my selection a little. But, in the end, I do tend to stick to the more traditional "big name" composers of that particular genre. I also try to look around a little bit – for instance, there's elements of minimalism in a lot of film soundtracks, so I try and see if there's anything current out there at the moment that students might actually be engaged with, then I try to see if I can use that repertoire if it's appropriate. Every year I go looking and kind of see what's out there.

'Styles my students at first might turn their noses up at are expressionism or maybe chance music, particularly twentieth-century styles. After a week or two of actually looking at it and deconstructing it, I always have a few students who are fascinated with it. These are students who are very much into popular music, don't listen to classical music and wouldn't have known who Schönberg or Stravinsky or any of these people would have been. And they end up actually choosing to compose in those styles, even though they have the option of doing something from a popular style.

'I had one student who did an amazing expressionist orchestral piece for their composition, and this student plays electric guitar and listens to heavy metal all the time. I think it might have got an A+. I was just amazed I think, because that's when I just went, "Wow – had we not looked at that in class would he ever have listened to that music? Would he ever have thought about going on the Internet and looking up Schönberg?" He wouldn't have known who that was.'

'So it's about opening the doors for them?', I ask

'It's about opening their minds. And letting the kids explore a little bit ... I think that there are things that need to be explored just to challenge them.

'I'm really big on including a massive variety of styles and genres. I really like to move through a lot of different repertoire. When I'm trying to teach a particular musical element I might use five or six different songs to do that. So half of the repertoire I use, I say, "OK this is good for them, they need to know it". And then the other half is really kind of up-to-date, what is current. At the same time I am being careful not to just use pop music. You know how there's a big debate about just putting pop music in because kids like it, but I think it's important to be actually learning something with it. I assess what I'm using: What's the context? What am I trying to achieve? If I could use a piece that's a little bit more relevant to them, maybe something off the charts, then I'll use that.

'This stems back to my experience at high school I think, because the most engaging and intriguing repertoire I ever came across was in Year 11 and 12 music. I think back to my own experience, and I never would have learned about that composer or that repertoire had I not done this in classroom music. I was really appreciative that I had the opportunity to be exposed to that.'

Jayden's reference to her own experience of being introduced to new repertoire through classroom music is highlighted in one particular lesson I observed, when she used one of the pieces that we studied together at school – 'A Survivor from Warsaw' by Schönberg. At the beginning of Jayden's Year 12 music lesson, she plays the students the recording, without discussion or introduction. The students are asked to recall the name of the piece and composer, which they do easily. When asked to describe and explain the musical features of the piece, they struggle, making seemingly random guesses at answers. Jayden guides them through the analysis with a series of closed questions. "Was the melody smooth or angular? Were the dynamics constant or did they change suddenly?"

This is the first time I have listened to this piece since I was in Year 12, some 14 years earlier. At the time, I remember feeling totally overwhelmed, by both the narrative and the music itself. I don't actually remember anything about the musical features of the work, only a feeling of discomfort and unease (although I do remember details of other studied works). When I listen to it now, in Jayden's classroom, I am able to focus on the musical features: I notice the *col legno* of the strings, the angular melodic ideas, the use of extremes of range, timbre and dynamics. As I listen to Jayden's students call out responses to her questions, it seems like they can't really hear the answers for themselves; they're trying to guess the answers rather than listen for them.

Jayden responds when she reads this later. 'Sometimes they are guessing. Often they want to give the responses that they think I want to hear, that they really try and please me. But I really push them to listen and think for themselves, I think that's more important than me telling them the right answers.

'I also really encourage the students to bring music in. With my Year 12s we were looking at fusion last week. And one of them put their hand up and said, "I've got a really awesome fusion song on my iPod." And it was this really random German opera/rock fusion. But one of the guys said, "I love this kind of stuff", which was great.

'Even my Grade 8 classes when we've done rock music, if they want to jump up and play songs while they're doing worksheets, they can. As long, obviously, as there's not swearing, it's fine. I mean every kid does have an iPod in their pocket, even if they're not meant to have them at school.

'Also, Year 8s can choose their repertoire to perform. I also have some beginner booklets that I made up myself, with really easy songs, song riffs by Rhianna, Blink 182 that only use three, four, five notes that I know beginners can do. They have that option, but if they don't want to do that option, there's a fantastic website that's full of riffs, that has sections for easy, intermediate and advanced. Usually they print it off at school and bring it to me to check – I have to approve it. And there are sometimes students who print off a song, come to me and say, "I just can't do it." And I say, "No, yes you can", and have them sit down with their pencil first and write the notes in, and just take their time. I tell them to start with one hand, and I might play the other part of the song while they do the bit they can do. There might be too many chords, so they might start with just two. It's just a really steady process.'

A respect for music and for each other

I ask Jayden what she wants the students to take away from classroom music, what she wants them to learn.

'Again, it sounds very clichéd, but a real appreciation, a real respect for music. And I'm really big on respecting one another and, I guess, building confidence. Whatever they're doing in the classroom, whether that's composing or performing or doing an assignment, I think it's important that they feel supported in a really good environment and gaining confidence with every task that they're doing.'

I ask Jayden to describe how she structures learning experiences to create this environment and to build their confidence.

'Well, I tend to really start early. I start it with my Grade 9s, and at the moment we're doing a World Music unit. At the start of the unit, I asked them to bring in music from their own culture, starting with questions like, "Who has a different cultural music they listen to at home? What culture? Do you speak a different language at home?" We go through all these things and most kids are really hesitant in the first lesson to actually say anything or share that kind of information because they, I think, are obviously worried about other kids laughing at them. I really, really push to promote that everyone is on equal footing and everyone's accepted and it doesn't matter the background. We're all equal. And really work hard on that just through my attitude and modelling how I respond to things and how I talk about different cultures. I really work, try and talk positively about every culture and sort of gain a respect for every different culture.

'I had a boy who I was sitting next to in the class (I was observing the lesson because I had a preservice teacher); he and I started chatting and he started to talk about what he was going to do for his prac assignment. "I don't know", he says. This is a student who's kind of usually a little bit disengaged with what's going on. So we just kept talking and then through a 15-minute conversation, I found out that he's got eight ukuleles at home and he's from the Cook Islands. And I'm like "wow!" Then he brought out his iPod and said, "Well, I can show you some of the songs that we listen to." So I'm at the back of the classroom sitting there listening to this native Cook Islands music, you know, and it's just fantastic. And now he's going to bring in his ukuleles and present to the class. So what I'm seeing is this gradual change, they're getting more comfortable.'

At a later time I ask Jayden whether this boy did bring his ukuleles in and play for the class.

'No, he never did. Apparently they're worth quite a lot of money and his parents wouldn't let him. I made some suggestions of how we could keep them safe, and I think it was partly laziness on his part. He's still in my class this year, and he's very hard to motivate; he really doesn't care much about anything. I haven't yet managed to get him to share that part of his culture with the class. He does play guitar for his prac performances, and he does quite well. He plays ukulele with his dad and his uncle, and I'm wondering whether it's something that he just wants to keep that separate from school.

'Then another student who was from South Africa – I didn't even know he was from South Africa for the whole first term. Then he got up and did a half-hour talk on South Africa. Not all about the music but just about the way he lived there. The class was totally engaged because talking about how he lived in a house with maids and the maids used to steal everything from them, and they had barbed wire around the house in case they got kidnapped, and these kids were just in awe of this story. I think he felt really good after he had done his little speech, because it took him a couple of weeks to gain the confidence.'

I'm somewhat startled by the racial undertones of this student's story, coloured by my own understanding of the racial tensions in South Africa. Jayden doesn't comment on it further at the time. At a later time, I ask her to reflect upon this story and how it encouraged the students to 'talk positively about every culture and sort of gain a respect for every different culture'.

She responds. 'I wanted to make an example of him for being courageous enough to share his story with the class. That's just his story, I can't really comment on that because that's his experience. You can't censor students from these things that are happening out there, and the fact that he was willing to share it, that's what I wanted to focus on.'

I can't help but wonder whether this is an example of a missed opportunity for a teachable moment.

Leaving the field

As I leave Seaview State High School, I note how different the music programme is from those I have observed in my other case sites. Seaview is a school that has embraced the diversity of the students and has sought to design ways for the students to participate in music education in a variety of ways. Recognising that many of the students aren't necessarily university bound, the school has made an effort to design a music programme that meets the needs of their clientele.

Jayden's classroom represents one of these pathways, the more academic option, which reflects her own musical background as a classically trained pianist. I am reminded frequently throughout my conversations with Jayden how strongly her own experiences as a student and as a learner shape her teaching practice. She draws inspiration from her own experience of music at high school, and what she would have liked to be a part of her music education. However, Jayden's students aren't all like her: they have different backgrounds, experiences and aspirations.

I wonder about how the students experience the multiple pathways that Seaview offers, whether all the pathways are visible to all students, or whether there is a sense of one pathway being 'not for the likes of me' (recall the discussion of Bourdieu's concept of habitus in Chapter 2). Matt and Jayden both claim that it's entirely up to the students which option they choose, but I wonder how the students see it, whether they see themselves as capable of continuing with the more academic courses. Jayden's comments regarding some of her more challenging classes, where many students were given failing grades, suggest that she assumes students who achieve poorly will not continue with music, regardless of whether they enjoy the class.

Note

1 This was later revised to Year 6, and at the time of writing, the Australian Curriculum: The Arts (ACARA, 2013) is 'available for use; awaiting final endorsement'.

Part III
Narratives illuminated

9 Capital, habitus and field in music education

Hierarchies, traditions and marginalisation

The discussion in this chapter will be through the lens of Bourdieu's relational sociology, particularly the concepts of habitus and field. As a precursor to this discussion, let us return to the basis premises from the literature in Chapters 3 and 4, which suggest:

1. music teachers' values and beliefs are developed through their socialisation within the field of music, most often Western art music;
2. these beliefs inform music teachers' propensity to treat secondary school music education as training for tertiary music studies;
3. practice of this nature is exclusionary and inappropriate, and should be replaced with practices that seek to provide a music education that has relevance for all students.

This chapter will be framed by these three premises, particularly considering the ways in which the narratives that this study produced align with them, and the evidence that represents points of departure, at times in small ways, and in others significantly. It will begin by exploring the ways in which the teachers' habitus was informed by the values of Western art music, and the ways in which this facilitated the doxa of this field being reproduced in their classrooms. Next, instances of resistance are explored, where the teachers deviate from these values, creating a culture of music making within the classroom that differs from the broader field. Finally, the chapter draws attention to moments of realisation that occurred during the course of this research, where the teachers saw the effects of their practice, as shaped by their habitus, differently.

Formation of the musical habitus: socialisation in the musical field

As the literature reviewed in Chapter 4 attests, music teachers' values and beliefs are shaped by their participation in the musical field, and for the vast majority of music teachers, this is primarily Western art music. This was the case for all four of the teachers in this study, to varying degrees. Michael and Jayden both completed degrees in performance; Jayden as a classical pianist, while Michael completed a classical degree, despite the fact that his instrument (saxophone) meant that his performing experience was mainly in jazz. Sam and Jan both learned piano while they were at school, although Sam also taught himself guitar and sang. Sam completed an arts degree with a double major in music, and he performed regularly in choral ensembles despite not being enrolled in a performance degree. Jan studied music and English at teachers' college, and has since completed a Masters degree in choral conducting.

While the teachers did not overtly adopt the values of Western art music in the most extreme depictions (as articulated by J. Mills, 1996; Ross, 1995; Small, 1998) as the values of the classroom, the classroom practice is shaped by these values, beliefs, norms and assumptions in important ways. In Sam's, Jan's and Jayden's classrooms, reading and writing of Western music notation was central to the way 'musicianship' is understood and some proficiency in the use of this notation was essential for success in the course. In spite of the fact that the Senior Syllabus (The State of Queensland, 2004) does not require student to demonstrate the use of notation, these three teachers felt it was important for the students to learn this skill, demonstrating the teachers' adherence to the doxa of Western art music that positions notation and the 'great works' as superior to other musical styles.

While there was evidence of the doxa of Western art music influencing the teachers' ideas about music and music education, these were not always the dominant values that informed the teachers' practice. In some cases (Michael and Jayden), values drawn from their own experiences of education were much more visible in their current practice than the values of traditional formal Western music learning. In the case of Sam and Jan, the institution of the individual school exerted a powerful influence over the way music is taught and learned, although it could be argued that these schools' values and beliefs are informed by traditions of Western art music.

Experiences as a student as informant of habitus

In all cases, significant elements of each teacher's values and beliefs were based on aspects of their own experience of school music education, either replicating their experiences of music and schooling as students (Michael and Jayden), or actively rejecting them (Sam). Sam's teaching practice was heavily influenced by his teacher preparation programme, and Jan's by her postgraduate education and in-service professional development.

This demonstrates the influence of the teachers' habitus on their classroom practice, which is shaped by their own experiences. The propensity for teachers to teach as they were taught at school is well documented in the literature (Cochran-Smith, 1991; Dolloff, 1999; Fenstermacher, 1978; Richardson, 1996, 2003; Richardson and Kile, 1999), casting doubt on the potential for preservice teacher education to make lasting changes in teachers' thinking.

Major and Palmer (2006) also found that some teachers base their practice on their own preferences as learners.

This was clearly seen in the practice of Michael, whose experience of informal learning environments inform his practice, and Jayden, who found her high school music classes so beneficial and enjoyable that she replicates many aspects in her own classroom. In contrast, Sam's practice is based on a conscious rejection of the approach he experienced at school. Despite enjoying music while he was at school, upon embarking on tertiary studies in music Sam felt that he was not well prepared. Sam's own high school music experiences were juxtaposed with what he saw in his teacher education, an approach that he immediately viewed as superior to what he had done at high school. Jan found that her music education and her teacher preparation programme did not equip her with adequate musical skills to develop the type of music programme that her principal demanded, so she sought out postgraduate study and professional development opportunities on which to base her practice.

In each of the cases, once the teacher had established an approach for their practice that aligned with their values and beliefs about music making, this changed very little. The pedagogy became practised and habitualised, with little evidence of questioning or reflecting upon their practice. As Benedict (2009) posits, unquestioning adoption of 'methods' or approaches has the potential to alienate both the teacher and students from music and music making. As described earlier, there are certainly cases where some students are alienated in the music classroom because their musical experiences and preferences were not valued. In some cases, while there was evidence of an increasing sense of reflection across the course of the research, the changes in thinking did not necessarily translate to changes in practice. This is discussed in more detail later in this chapter (see 'Unpacking the habitus', below).

High-brow culture: the values of the subfield of restricted production in music education

In each of the narratives, there is evidence of the values of the elite subfield prevailing over the content and pedagogy of the music classroom, and also some points of departure, where the classroom values differ from those of Western classical music, at times in small ways and at others significantly. This section explores the ways in which the values that dictate the acceptable behaviours and the knowledge and skills that are considered worthwhile contribute to a multi-faceted hierarchy of students and musics.

Notation

Notation was a topic of discussion, at times contentious, in all of the interviews, with each of the teachers holding a strong view on the role of notation in music education. To situate this within a broader context, the Senior Syllabus (Years 11 and 12; 16-plus) for Music (The State of Queensland,

2004) was a significant curriculum change from the previous syllabus (The State of Queensland, 1995), removing the need to test aural dictation skills, assess compositions handwritten in traditional notation, sight-read, submit notation of works performed and analyse from a written score. There was an increase in the level of choice for students about how they demonstrate their musical competence: traditional score, graphic score or audio file for presenting compositions; aural or visual analysis; and perform with or without a written score.

In Sam's, Jan's and Jayden's classrooms, reading and writing of Western music notation was central to the way 'musicianship' is understood and some proficiency in the use of this notation was essential for success in the course. In spite of the fact that the Senior Syllabus (The State of Queensland, 2004) does not require student to demonstrate the use of notation, these three teachers felt it was important for the students to learn this skill, demonstrating the teachers' adherence to the doxa of Western art music that positions notation and the 'great works' as superior to other musical styles.

In Michael's classroom, the same emphasis on the importance of notation wasn't evident. Michael raised the question of teaching notation in the music classroom, an issue that he returned to repeatedly throughout our conversations. Although he feels the need to assure me that he *himself* reads very well, he does not believe it is possible for students to develop fluent reading skills in the time available for classroom music so he chooses to focus on other ways of recording and communicating musical ideas. While Michael says he is happy with the choices he has made, his repeated return to this topic to elaborate on his justification might be viewed as a form of defence.

Technique

The importance of good technique is another value that features in the field of Western art music. Linking back to ideas about the importance of notation, Jayden's describes why she thinks technique is so important.

> I really want to teach them the right technique, because when they go home and I'm not there to look over their shoulder, then they're not playing the keyboard with one finger and they should be able to try to play harder songs. So by setting them up with the right hand position, they should be able to find a song that uses the same notes and play it successfully.
>
> There is one boy who is going onto YouTube, as there's a guy who posts videos on how to learn the piano. So he's been watching and learning visually from these YouTube videos. To me that's not ideal, obviously, because I come from a classical piano background ... But that's still a success, because he's engaged ... I don't mind how he's doing it, but then I'll have to go and correct his technique. ... I think there's problems down the track ... are they limiting themselves by learning things on YouTube

and not developing the right technique, not learning to read?

Jayden's comments here illuminate her beliefs around the importance of the teacher as director of the learning, as the possessor of knowledge. This points to a view of knowledge as fixed, and the purpose of education as the transmission of that knowledge.

Students' musics on the margins

All four teachers drew attention to the differences between formal music education and music making that the students participated in at school and their more informal musical experiences outside. There was evidence in all four classrooms of the teachers' efforts to encourage the students to be more open about their musical choices outside the classroom. Jayden commented on this explicitly.

> I look at the clientele that I have and seeing what styles they're into, and trying to expose them to things that I think they would never ever listen to ... It's about opening their minds. And letting the kids explore a little bit ... I think that there are things that need to be explored just to challenge them.

The idea of classroom music providing the students with experience of different types of music to ones that they would choose to pursue on their own was reiterated by all of the teachers at various times. In all classrooms, the teacher selected the majority of the repertoire to be studied, with opportunities for students to choose music that interests them some of the time (Michael and Jayden) or infrequently (Jan and Sam). Some of the students felt that the music that they liked was not welcome in the music classroom.

There were two students in particular who felt that their musical experiences didn't hold value for their music teacher: Isabel at Chiswick College and James at Blackfield State High School. Both of these students were academically high-achieving students, not the usual students to be on the fringe of classroom experiences.

Isabel had just joined her class this year, for her final year at school, but she had been involved in the extra-curricular music programme throughout her time at Chiswick College, playing piano and flute. She professes to love classroom music, particularly composition, for which she has a particular flair. However, in addition to playing Western classical instruments, Isabel also plays a Korean flute called a 'danso', an instrument that she has never brought to school or discussed with her music teacher.

This illustrates the Eurocentric conceptualisation of music that exists within the music classroom, an attitude that would not be considered unique or unusual in many schools. At Chiswick College, it is the belief in the superiority of the music itself that is maintained. Western art music is positioned as the yardstick by which all musics are measured. While the pedagogical practice is built around a premise of making this music literacy accessible to all students, even the most musically inexperienced, Western music remains privileged over other styles and genres, including the musics from the cultural backgrounds of the students.

In James's case, he describes his experience in pop music and his lack of musical theory knowledge as a problem for him in the music classroom. He describes how he fears the composition task where he'll need to 'somehow figure out how to write it, an orchestral or like a string quartet or something like that. Like a piece that's classical.' This is despite the state-wide curriculum for Year 12 music (The State of Queensland, 2004) explicitly making provisions for students to present assessment tasks that are within styles or genres with which they are comfortable. For James, his marginalisation came from his feelings of isolation from his peers as well as his teacher, as the majority of the other students were more comfortable using notation and working within a classical idiom.

There is a significant body of literature developing around the value of connecting students' in- and out-of-school musical worlds. This issue is not the focus of the chapter, but provides an example of how knowledge of particular types is a form of symbolic capital that can be the basis of transactions for students to improve their position within the classroom.

Points of departure: deviating from the values of the elite subfield

Talent and music making

As described in Chapter 3, the belief that music making requires talent forms a significant part of the doxa within the fields of various Western musical styles (Kingsbury, 1988; Koza, 2001; Small, 1998). However, all of the teachers in this study agreed that all students are capable of making music – composing, singing and playing instruments – as part of the classroom programme. This belief represents a departure from the presumption that music making necessarily requires innate talent, a belief that is widely held in Western cultures (Kingsbury, 1988; Koza, 2001; Small, 1998).

The students in each of the classrooms were active participants in many facets of music making, including singing and playing instruments, composing and improvising. The balance between these activities varied in each school, according to the teacher's pedagogical approach and/or the interests and desires of the students (self-determined and/or identified by the teacher). In all of the programmes, students in Year 8 learn an instrument as a class (one or more of keyboard, guitar, drums and recorder), being given the option of continuing this learning in later years or playing an instrument that they learn outside the classroom programme. In Sam's classroom, much of the music making was through whole-class singing, while in Michael's and Jan's classroom it was usually through playing instruments individually or in small groups. Students in Jayden's classroom were seen composing and improvising in groups.

The practices observed in these classrooms are at odds with some of the suggestions made in the literature about the elitist tendencies of music teachers (particularly Mills, 1996; Ross, 1995). In these classrooms, there is a different view of what it means to be a 'performer': there is a belief that all students are capable of singing, playing and composing, but the purposes of their singing, playing and composing are different from those of 'professionalised' musical fields. There is an emphasis on learning through engaging in music making rather than music making for the purposes of creating a 'product' (conflating 'music' and 'musical works'). The study of musical works also occurred in each of the classrooms, and the proportions of time spent on singing, playing, composing, improvising, listening and analysing varied in each site. There was, however, an underlying sense that students were positioned as being capable of participating in music making, rather than being limited or relegated to the role of 'educated audience member'.

As a caveat to this, some of the teachers suggested there were limits to how successfully some students would achieve in music, based on their prior experiences of music education in and out of school. Sam suggested that it was very difficult for students who entered the programme at Chiswick later than Year 8, because of the way that the pedagogical approach builds a specific set of language, skills and understandings, some of which aren't developed in other approaches to music learning. Jan suggested that students who have never taken lessons (in singing or an instrument) outside of the classroom programme might struggle to succeed at the Senior Music level (Year 11 and 12), but that all students who approach their work diligently were capable of achieving passing grades. Jan suggested that this limit on their achievement deterred some academically high-achieving students from taking music.

> There's such a strong focus on academic excellence and achievement here that some students who are very bright but maybe don't have a lot of musical experience feel like they won't achieve at as high a level as they might want to. I had a student a few years ago who was very capable, very bright, but she wasn't going to top the class. And she knew that if she took biology she could.

These comments from Sam and Jan draw attention to the differences between music and some other academic disciplines. A discipline that is characterised by formal instruction outside of the school setting (such as music, dance and sports) creates a divide between students who have had the opportunity and support necessary to participate in such programmes and those who have not. In Jayden's and Michael's classrooms, there were more students whose experience of singing and playing was developed in informal settings (peer- or self-taught), but there was still a sense that the knowledges and skills that are developed in formal music instructional settings being positioned as more valuable, as the easiest path to success with the classroom programme.

An embracing of mass-culture: Michael at St Mark's

The most significant departure from 'traditional' approaches to music education (which is heavily influenced by the elite subfield) could be seen in Michael's music classroom at St Mark's, in terms of both pedagogy and content. As discussed earlier in this chapter, the explicit teaching of notation was minimal. The students were given a high degree of choice in what they sing, play, compose and analyse, and indeed, how they spend their lesson time. This informal approach was instinctive for Michael, although it aligns with Lucy Green's ideas on informal learning and popular music pedagogy.[1] Michael felt that the students 'need time to explore, so here we give them time and space', and thus his approach deviated from the teacher-centred pedagogy commonly associated with the elite subfield.

Unpacking the habitus: moments of illumination

An unanticipated outcome of the research was the growth experienced by some of the teachers as a result of the opportunities to reflect as part of the research process. While reflection has long been considered a crucial aspect of professional growth, the time and space, as well as the provision of external feedback on their reflections, are not always available to teachers. The opportunity to participate in professional conversation about their values and beliefs was a new experience for all of the teachers. Most significantly, several teachers began to question why they do what they do, raising new questions in response to reading my interpretations.

Sam

Sam describes his interaction with Jess, a student who entered his classroom with a different expectation of what classroom music was about.
July 2009

> Jess didn't like that she was – I don't want to say forced – but regularly encouraged to sing. That made her feel very uncomfortable despite doing very well at it and I continued to praise her for the efforts that she was making. I thought that I'd tried to make her comfortable but that is a process that can take some time, and in the end I respect that she didn't want to join in. At her old school Jess's experience in music had been similar to my own: to pick up a guitar and learn to play chords in the classroom and she had loved that in the past and I just don't do that in my classroom.

I'd spent the whole of first semester encouraging her to stay with it, and she was achieving quite well, sitting on a B, which is a high achievement for somebody who's come into Grade 10 music with the inability to read staff notation. I mean, there are many positives: she left [the subject] knowing how to read the treble clef, which she didn't know how to do when she came in. She left with an understanding of how rhythm works and she hadn't in the past.

The following year, Sam took leave without pay from Chiswick College to travel and work overseas. As we reviewed the interim research texts via email, he made these comments in reference to the previous extract.
February 2011

I read this and I think to myself: where is the consideration for her simply enjoying herself in the classroom? Where have I tried to make an effort for her to have a little of what she was used to in my classroom? While I was encouraging and sympathetic to her concerns I didn't change the way I taught: that seems like a failure to offer her an opportunity that could have flourished.

Sam's commitment to the doxa of the field – in this case, music education in the context of how it is taught at Chiswick College – contributed to the stability of Sam's habitus, and a continual process of reproduction of the status quo. Sam's commitment to the doxa was so strong that he had not considered the possibility of modifying his practice to accommodate Jess's (or any of his students') desires or preferences, and this behaviour was sanctioned by the subfield. The 'needs' of students are predetermined by the teachers, both past and present.

It is important to acknowledge the particular circumstances that led to this change in Sam's thinking about his practice. During the process of composing, re-composing and editing this research text, Sam began to see his own practice in a different light. One might say he caught his first glimpse of his past failure to see another way of doing things. For Sam, this process of recognition occurred in very specific circumstances. His departure from the subfield (Chiswick College) to the larger field of music education that accepts a wider range of pedagogies and practices opened his eyes to the choices that were invisible before. In addition to this, the prompts Sam received as a participant in this research project were a catalyst for a deeper level of reflection. The moment of realisation occurred almost a year after the event, after several recursive iterations through reviewing and discussing the text. In previous iterations, Sam had defended his pedagogical choices, claiming that he didn't think that's what students need in the music classroom. The 'meta-reflection' that Sam undertook as he read the manuscript drafts would likely not have occurred had he not been a participant in the research.

Jan

As someone who has been teaching for 30 years, Jan's ideas about teaching music are based on her practice over a long period. One of the difficulties she identified in our first interview was associated with engaging Year 8 students who had not learned music before. She stated, 'If they wanted to do music they would have done it in primary school.'

> I don't really love teaching Year 8 – because it's compulsory there are so many kids who have decided from primary school that they don't like music … It's really hard when they come from the primary school with preconceived ideas. Also, if they had wanted to do music they would have done it by now. I was a great believer in this 'music for all' when I started going to the [Kodály] Summer School and I really thought, 'This is right!' But then I got back to the reality of it and I'm like, there are some kids who simply are not interested.

As I described in Chapter 7, I couldn't reconcile these comments with what I saw in her classroom. She was firm with the students, but warm and engaging, and all of the students participated compliantly in all aspects of the lesson. When I commented on how much I enjoyed her Year 8 students, she was quick to clarify her comments, telling me 'None of that really applied to the classes you observed. Those Year 8 classes were some of the best I've ever had.'

The ideas that Jan expressed to me in our initial interview were based on practice of the past rather than the present. Her statements about teaching Year 8 represented attitudes that she had perhaps not reflected on in light of her current teaching context. Through the research process, by reading the interim research texts and through our conversations and interviews that probed the ideas she originally expressed, the tension between her beliefs and her experience was tested. This could be termed what Clandinin *et al.* (2006) call a 'bumping place', a tension that causes a story to be shifted, changed or interrupted (p. 36). Although these authors typically use 'bumping places' to refer to the tensions between the experiences and stories of different people, this tension was an internal bumping place for Jan, one which she was able to resolve through participation in the research process.

The professional growth which these teachers demonstrated by participating in the research process has the potential to inform teacher professional development programmes. All of the teachers actively sought professional learning experiences, although none had ever engaged in professional conversations about their values and beliefs prior to participating in this study. The importance of teachers' reflecting on their practice has been well documented in the literature (Calderhead, 1989; Loughran, 2002; Schön, 1987), however, as Loughran (2002) identifies, not all reflection leads to valuable learning. The strength of this approach is that it relies on *reflective dialogue*;

the process of discussing reflections led to greater depth of thinking from the teachers. In addition, conversing with a professional colleague who was not a co-worker or employer meant that there was a safe space for the teachers to tell their stories. The stories presented here highlight the potential for similar processes to be adopted as part of a professional development programme for teachers.

In closing

This chapter seeks to synthesise the ideas presented in the earlier parts of this book, drawing together the ideas from the literature and the narratives, and illuminating ideas through the lens of Bourdieu's theory of practice. By exploring the way the doxa of the field of music, particularly of Western art music, influence school music education, we can see how these ideas privilege particular experiences and backgrounds – capitals of both students and teachers – over others.

Evidence of the 'problems' with music education and music teachers in schools that are described in the literature can certainly be seen in the narratives presented in this book. However, there is also evidence of teachers breaking away from these ideas, and this is captured in the nuance and complexity of their stories. The literature on music teachers and music teacher education doesn't always recognise the diversity of experiences, or provide illustrations of how things might be done differently.

However, a Bourdieuian analysis is not an end in itself. It provides a means of seeing things differently, to allow for a reshaping of existing practices. An unanticipated but powerful outcome of the research was the level of personal and professional growth demonstrated by some of the participants through the research process. While all teachers hold values and beliefs that shape their practice, not all teachers engage in a process of self-reflection and unpack these in the ways that the teacher participants did in this study. In my final meetings with each of the teachers, I noticed an increased level of clarity to their thoughts, where they began to question their practices, or develop more sophisticated justifications for their choices. The scope of the project did not allow for longitudinal investigation of the lasting impact of these reflections, and whether they led to discernible changes in practice, or whether they remained as an uncomfortable tension, a schism between habitus and their practice.

It becomes clear through stories told in this book that teachers' personal experiences, values and beliefs have a significant impact on how curriculum is enacted, that the choices different teachers make serve (or don't serve) the needs and interests of different students. Further, the book highlights the potential for teachers to become aware of these forces and, perhaps, make changes that would provide a more inclusive experience of music education for their students.

Note

1 Michael was not aware of Green's work or the Musical Futures initiative at the time the fieldwork was conducted. The first pilots of Musical Futures Australia began in 2010, after the interviews and member checking was completed.

References

Abramo, J.M. 2009. Popular music and gender in the classroom. Unpublished dissertation, Teachers College, New Columbia University, New York.

Adler, A. and Harrison, S.D. 2004. Swinging back the gender pendulum: Addressing boys' needs in music education research and practice. *In* L. Bartel ed. *Research to practice: Questioning the music education paradigm.* Toronto: International Society for Music Education, pp. 270–89.

Allsup, R.E. 2010. Choosing music literature. *In* H.F. Abeles and L.A. Custodero eds. *Critical issues in music education: Contemporary theory and practice.* New York: Oxford University Press, pp. 215–35.

Allsup, R.E. and Olson, N.J. 2012. New educational frameworks for popular music and informal learning. *In* S. Karlsen and L. Väkevä eds. *Future prospects for music education: Corroborating informal learning pedagogy.* Newcastle upon Tyne: Cambridge Scholars Publishing, pp. 11–22.

Alperson, P. 1991. What should one expect from a philosophy of music education? *Journal of Aesthetic Education* 25(3): 215–42.

Australian Curriculum Assessment and Reporting Authority. 2011. *MySchool* [online]. Available at: www.myschool.edu.au [accessed 9 September 2011].

Bailey, B.A. and Davidson, J.W. 2002. Adaptive characteristics of group singing: Perceptions from members of a choir for homeless men. *Musicae Scientiae* 6(2): 221–56.

Ballantyne, J. and Mills, C. 2008. Promoting socially just and inclusive music teacher education: Exploring perceptions of early-career teachers. *Research Studies in Music Education* 30(1): 77–91.

Barone, T. 2000. *Aesthetics, politics and educational inquiry: Essays and examples.* New York: Peter Lang.

Barone, T. 2001. *Touching eternity: The enduring outcomes of teaching.* New York: Teachers College Press.

Barone, T. 2009. Narrative researchers as witnesses of injustice and agents of social change? *Educational Researcher* 38(8): 591–7.

Barrett, M.S. and Stauffer, S.L. 2009. Narrative inquiry: From story to method. *In* M.S. Barrett and S.L. Stauffer eds. *Narrative inquiry in music education: Troubling certainty.* London: Springer, pp. 7–18.

Benedict, C. 2009. Processes of alienation: Marx, Orff and Kodaly. *British Journal of Music Education* 26(2): 213–24.

Bennett, T., Emmison, M. and Frow, J. 1999. *Accounting for tastes: Everyday Australian cultures.* Cambridge: Cambridge University Press.

Bernard, R. 2004. A dissonant duet: Discussions of music teaching and music making. *Music Education Research* 6(3): 281–98.

Blacking, J. 1973. *How musical is man?* Seattle: University of Washington Press.

Bouij, C. 2004. Two theoretical perspectives on the socialization of music teachers. *Action, criticism and theory for music education* [online]. Available at: http://act. maygroup.org/articles/Bouij3_3.pdf [accessed 30 May 2008].

Bourdieu, P. 1977. *Outline of a theory of practice*. Cambridge: Cambridge University Press.

Bourdieu, P. 1984. *Distinction: A social critique of the judgement of taste*. Cambridge, MA: Harvard University Press.

Bourdieu, P. 1986. Forms of capital. *In* J.G. Richardson ed. *Handbook of theory and research for the sociology of education*. New York: Greenwood Press, pp. 241–58.

Bourdieu, P. 1989. Social space and symbolic power. *Sociological Theory* 7(1): 14–25.

Bourdieu, P. 1990. *The logic of practice*. 2nd edn. Stanford, CA: Stanford University Press.

Bourdieu, P. 1993a. *The field of cultural production: Essays on art and literature*. New York: Columbia University Press.

Bourdieu, P. 1993b. *Sociology in Question*. London: Sage.

Bourdieu, P. 1998. *Practical Reason*. Stanford, CA: Stanford University Press.

Bourdieu, P. 1999. Understanding. *In* P. Bourdieu, ed. *The weight of the world: Social suffering in contemporary society*. Stanford, CA: Stanford University Press, pp. 607–26.

Bourdieu, P. 2005. *The social structures of the economy*. Cambridge: Polity Press.

Bourdieu, P. and Passeron, J. 1990. *Reproduction in education, society and culture*. 2nd edn. London: Sage.

Bourdieu, P. and Wacquant, L.J.D. 1992. *An invitation to reflexive sociology*. Cambridge: Polity Press.

Bowman, W.D. 1991. An essay review of Bennett Reimer's 'A philosophy of music education'. *Quarterly Journal of Music Teaching and Learning* 2(3): 76–87.

Bowman, W.D. 1993. The problem of aesthetics and multiculturalism in music education. *Canadian Music Educator* 34(5): 23–30.

Bowman, W.D. 2007a. Who is the 'We'? Rethinking professionalism in music education. *Action, Criticism and Theory for Music Education* [online]. Available at: http://act. maydaygroup.org/articles/Bowman6_4.pdf [accessed 9 May 2009].

Bowman, W.D. 2007b. Who's asking? (Who's answering?) Theorizing social justice in music education. *Action, Criticism and Theory for Music Education* [online]. Available at: http://act.maydaygroup.org/articles/BowmanEditorial6_4.pdf [accessed 21 April 2008].

Bowman, W.D. 2010. No one true way: Music education without redemptive truth. *In* T.A. Regelski and J.T. Gates eds. *Music education for changing times: Guiding visions for practice*. Dordrecht, The Netherlands: Springer, pp. 3–16.

Bradley, D. 2006. Music education, multiculturalism, and anti-racism: Can we talk? *Action, Criticism and Theory for Music Education* [online]. Available at: http://act. maydaygroup.org/articles/Bradley5_2.pdf [accessed 3 March 2009].

Bradley, D. 2007. The sounds of silence: Talking race in music education. *Action, Criticism and Theory for Music Education* [online]. Available at: http://act.maydaygroup. org/articles/Bradley6_4.pdf [accessed 29 May 2008].

Bradley, D. 2012. Good for what, good for whom? Decolonizing music education philosophies. *In* W.D. Bowman and A.L. Frega eds. *The Oxford handbook of philosophy in music education*. New York: Oxford University Press, pp. 409–33.

Bray, D. 2000. An examination of GCSE music uptake rates. *British Journal of Music Education* 17(01): 79–89.

Bray, D. 2009. *Creating a musical school*. Oxford: Oxford University Press.

Calderhead, J. 1989. Reflective teaching and teacher education. *Teaching and Teacher Education* 5(1): 43–51.

Chanan, M. 1994. *Musica practica: The social practice of Western music from Gregorian chant to postmodernism*. London: Verso.

Clandinin, D.J. 2010. Potentials and possibilities for narrative inquiry. *In* L.K. Thompson and M.R. Campbell eds. *Issues of identity in music education*. Charlotte, NC: Information Age Publishing, pp. 1–14.

Clandinin, D.J. and Connelly, F.M. 2000. *Narrative inquiry: Experience and story in qualitative research*. San Francisco: Jossey-Bass.

Clandinin, D.J. and Murphy, M.S. 2009. Relational ontological commitments in narrative inquiry. *Educational Researcher* 38(8): 598–602.

Clandinin, D.J. and Rosiek, J. 2007. Mapping a landscape of narrative inquiry: Borderland spaces and tensions. *In* D.J. Clandinin ed. *Handbook of narrative inquiry: Mapping a methodology*. Thousand Oaks, CA: Sage, pp. 35–76.

Clandinin, D.J. *et al.* 2006. *Composing diverse identities: Narrative inquiries into the interwoven lives of children and teachers*. New York: Routledge.

Clements, A.C. 2012. Escaping the classical canon: Changing methods through a change in paradigm. *In* S. Karlsen and L. Väkevä eds. *Future prospects for music education: Corroborating informal learning pedagogy*. Newcastle upon Tyne: Cambridge Scholars Publishing, pp. 3–10.

Cochran-Smith, M. 1991. Reinventing student teaching. *Journal of Teacher Education* 42(2): 104–18.

Connelly, F.M. and Clandinin, D.J. 2006. Narrative inquiry. *In* J.L. Green, G. Camilli and P.B. Elmore eds. *Handbook of complementary methods in educational research*. Washington, DC: American Educational Research Association, pp. 477–88.

Denzin, N.K. 1978. *The research act: A theoretical introduction to sociological methods*. 2nd edn. New York: McGraw-Hill.

Denzin, N.K. and Lincoln, Y.S. 2003. *Collecting and interpreting qualitative materials*. Thousand Oaks, CA: Sage.

Dolloff, L.A. 1999. Imagining ourselves as teachers: The development of teacher identity in music teacher education. *Music Education Research* 1(2): 191–207.

Dwyer, R. (2015). Unpacking the habitus: Exploring a music teacher's values, beliefs and practices. *Research Studies in Music Education* 37(1): 93–106. doi:10.1177/1321103X15589260

Elliott, D.J. 1995. *Music matters*. New York: Oxford University Press.

Ericsson, K.A. 2006. The influence of experience and deliberate practice on the development of superior expert performance. *In* K.A. Ericsson *et al.* eds. *The Cambridge handbook of expertise and expert performance*. Cambridge: Cambridge University Press, pp. 685–705.

Fairchild, C. 2007. Building the authentic celebrity: The 'Idol' phenomenon in the attention economy. *Popular Music and Society* 30(3): 355–75.

Fenstermacher, G.D. 1978. A philosophical consideration of recent research on teacher effectiveness. *Review of Research in Education* 6: 157–85.

Freire, P. 1972. *Pedagogy of the oppressed*. Harmondsworth: Penguin Books.

Gale, T. and Densmore, K. 2000. *Just schooling: Explorations in the cultural politics of teaching*. Buckingham: Open University Press.

Gammon, V. 1996. What is wrong with school music? A response to Malcolm Ross. *British Journal of Music Education* 13: 101–22.

Gardner, H. 1983. *Frames of mind: The theory of multiple intelligences*. New York: Basic Books.

Gates, J.T. 2010. Introduction: Grounding music education in changing times. *In* T.A. Regelski and J.T. Gates eds. *Music education for changing times: Guiding visions for practice*. Dordrecht, The Netherlands: Springer, pp. xix–xxx.

Gould, E. 2012. Uprooting music education pedagogies and curricula: Becoming-musician and the Deleuzian refrain. *Discourse: Studies in the Cultural Politics of Education* 33(1): 75–86.

Green, L. 1997. *Music, gender, education*. Cambridge: Cambridge University Press.

Green, L. 1999. Research in the sociology of music education: Some introductory concepts. *Music Education Research* 1(2): 159–70.

Green, L. 2001. Music in society and education. *In* C. Philpott and C. Plummeridge eds. *Issues in music education*. London: RoutledgeFalmer, pp. 47–60.

Green, L. 2002a. From the Western classics to the world: Secondary music teachers' changing attitudes in England, 1982 and 1998. *British Journal of Music Education* 19(1): 5–30.

Green, L. 2002b. *How popular musicians learn: A way ahead for music education*. Burlington, VT: Ashgate.

Green, L. 2008. *Music, informal learning and the school: A new classroom pedagogy*. Farnham: Ashgate.

Gudmundsdottir, S. 1996. The teller, the tale, and the one being told: The narrative nature of the research interview. *Curriculum Inquiry* 26(3): 293–306.

Hargreaves, D.J., Purves, R.M., Welch, G.F. and Marshall, N.A. 2007. Developing identities and attitudes in musicians and classroom music teachers. *British Journal of Educational Psychology* 77: 665–82.

Harrison, S.D. 2001. Real men don't sing. *Australian Voice* 11: 31–6.

Harrison, S.D. 2003. Music versus sport: What's the score? *Australian Journal of Music Education* 1: 10–15.

Harrison, S.D. 2008. *Masculinities and music*. Newcastle upon Tyne: Cambridge Scholars Publishing.

Harrison, S.D. 2009. Aussie blokes and music. *In* S.D. Harrison ed. *Male voices: Stories of boys learning through music making*. Camberwell, Victoria: ACER Press.

Hatch, J.A. 2002. *Doing qualitative research in educational settings*. Albany: State University of New York Press.

Heidegren, C.-G. and Lundberg, H. 2010. Towards a sociology of philosophy. *Acta Sociologica* 53(1): 3–18.

House of Representatives, Standing Committee on Education and Training 2002. *Boys: Getting it right*. Canberra: Parliament of the Commonwealth of Australia.

Jorgensen, E.R. 2003. Western classical music and general education. *Philosophy of Music Education Review* 11(2): 130–9.

Jørgensen, H. 2000. Student learning in higher instrumental education: Who is responsible? *British Journal of Music Education* 17(1): 67–77.

Jorquera Jaramillo, M.C. 2008. The music educator's professional knowledge. *Music Education Research* 10(3): 347–59.

Juntunen, M.-L. and Westerlund, H. 2011. The legacy of music education methods in teacher education: The metanarrative of Dalcroze Eurythmics as a case. *Research Studies in Music Education* 33(1): 47–58.

Karlsen, S. and Väkevä, L., eds. 2012. *Future prospects for music education: Corroborating informal learning pedagogy.* Newcastle upon Tyne: Cambridge Scholars Publishing.

Kingsbury, H. 1988. *Music, talent, and performance.* Philadelphia: Temple University Press.

Koza, J. 1993. The 'missing males' and other gender issues in music education: Evidence from the *Music Supervisors' Journal*, 1914–1924. *Journal of Research in Music Education* 41(3): 212–32.

Koza, J. 2001. Multicultural approaches to music education. *In* C.A. Grant and M.L. Gomez eds. *Campus and classroom: Making schooling multicultural.* Upper Saddle River, NJ: Prentice-Hall.

Lamont, A., Hargreaves, D.J., Marshall, N. and Tarrant, M. 2003. Young people's music in and out of school. *British Journal of Music Education* 20(3): 229–41.

Lamont, A. and Maton, K. 2010. Unpopular music: Beliefs and behaviours towards music in education. *In* R. Wright ed. *Sociology and music education.* Farnham: Ashgate, pp. 63–80.

Langer, S.K. 1953. *Feeling and form.* New York: Charles Scribner's Sons.

Lehmann, A.C. and Ericsson, K.A. 1997. Research on expert performance and deliberate practice: Implications for the education of amateur musicians and music students. *Psychomusicology: A Journal of Research in Music Cognition* 16(1–2): 40–58.

Lehmann, A.C., Sloboda, J.A. and Woody, R.H. 2007. *Psychology for musicians: Understanding and acquiring the skills.* New York: Oxford University Press.

Levine, L.W. 1988. *Highbrow/lowbrow: The emergence of cultural hierarchy in America.* Cambridge, MA: Harvard University Press.

Lingard, B., Martino, W. and Mills, M. 2009. *Boys and schooling: Beyond structural reform.* Basingstoke: Palgrave Macmillan.

Loughran, J.J. 2002. Effective reflective practice: In search of meaning in learning about teaching. *Journal of Teacher Education* 53(1): 33–43.

Major, C. and Palmer, B. 2006. Reshaping teaching and learning: The transformation of faculty pedagogical content knowledge. *Higher Education* 51(4): 619–47.

Mateiro, T. and Westvall, M. 2013. The cultural dimensions of music teachers' professional knowledge. *In* E. Georgii-Hemming, P. Burnard and S.E. Holgersen eds. *Professional knowledge in music teacher education.* Farnham: Ashgate, pp. 157–72.

Maton, K. 2008. Habitus. *In* M. Grenfell ed. *Pierre Bourdieu: Key concepts.* Durham: Acumen, pp. 49–66.

McCarthy, M. and Goble, J.S. 2002. Music education philosophy: Changing times. *Music Educators Journal* 89(1): 19–23.

McEwan, R.W. 2006. Student motivation to participate in an elective classroom music curriculum: A case study of the multi-dimensional aspects of participation and motivation. Unpublished doctoral dissertation, Faculty of Education, University of Tasmania.

Merriam, A.P. 1964. *The anthropology of music.* Evanston, IL: North-Western University Press.

Merriam, A.P. 1967. *The ethnomusicology of the Flathead Indians.* Chicago: Aldine.

Messenger, J. 1958. Esthetic talent. *Basic College Quarterly* 4: 20–4.

Meyer, L.B. 1956. *Emotion and meaning in music.* Chicago: University of Chicago Press.

Mills, C. 2012. When 'picking the right people' is not enough: A Bourdieuian analysis of social justice and dispositional change in pre-service teachers. *International Journal of Educational Research* 53: 269–77.

Mills, J. 1996. Starting secondary school. *British Journal of Music Education* 13: 5–14.

Moore, R. 2008. Capital. *In* M. Grenfell ed. *Pierre Bourdieu: Key concepts.* Durham: Acumen, pp. 101–18.

Mulhall, A. 2003. In the field: Notes on observation in qualitative research. *Journal of Advanced Nursing* 41(3): 306–13.

Nettl, B. 1989. Mozart and the ethnomusicological study of Western culture (An essay in four movements). *Yearbook for Traditional Music* 21: 1–16.

Nettl, B. 2007. An ethnomusicological perspective. *In* L. Bresler ed. *International handbook of research in arts education.* Dordrecht, The Netherlands: Springer, pp. 829–34.

Noddings, N. 2005. *The challenge to care in schools: An alternative approach to education.* 2nd edn. New York: Teachers College Press.

Ollerenshaw, J.A. and Creswell, J.W. 2002. Narrative research: A comparison of two restorying data analysis approaches. *Qualitative Inquiry* 8: 329–47.

Pajares, M.F. 1992. Teachers' beliefs and educational research: Cleaning up a messy construct. *Review of Educational Research* 62(3): 307–32.

Parker, A. 1996. The construction of masculinity within boys' physical education. *Gender and Education* 8(2) 141–57.

Philpott, C. 2010. The sociological critique of curriculum music in England: Is radical change really possible? *In* R. Wright ed. *Sociology and music education.* Farnham: Ashgate, pp. 81–92.

Pinnegar, S. and Daynes, J.G. 2007. Locating narrative inquiry historically: Thematics in the turn to narrative. *In* D.J. Clandinin ed. *Handbook of narrative inquiry: Mapping a methodology.* Thousand Oaks, CA: Sage, pp. 3–34.

Plummer, D. 1999. *One of the boys: Masculinity, homophobia and modern manhood.* New York: Harrington.

Plummeridge, C. 1997. The rights and wrongs of school music: A brief comment on Malcolm Ross's paper. *British Journal of Music Education* 14: 23–7.

Polkinghorne, D.E. 1995. Narrative configuration in qualitative analysis. *International Journal of Qualitative Studies in Education* 8(1): 5–23.

Pollack, W. 1999. *Real boys.* New York: Holt.

Regelski, T.A. 1997. Musicians, teachers and the social construction of reality. *In* R. Rideout ed. *On the sociology of music education.* Norman: University of Oklahoma, School of Music, pp. 95–111.

Regelski, T.A. 1998. Critical theory as a foundation for critical thinking in music education. *Studies in Music from the University of Western Ontario* 17(4): 1–21.

Regelski, T.A. 2012. Musicianism and the ethics of school music. *Action, Criticism and Theory for Music Education* 11(1): 7–42.

Reimer, B. 1970. *A philosophy of music education.* Englewood Cliffs, NJ: Prentice Hall.

Reimer, B. 1989a. Music education as aesthetic education: Past and present. *Music Educators Journal* 75(6): 22–8.

Reimer, B. 1989b. Music education as aesthetic education: Toward the future. *Music Educators Journal* 75(7): 26–32.

Reimer, B. 1989c. *A philosophy of music education.* 2nd edn. Englewood Cliffs, NJ: Prentice Hall.

Reimer, B. 1997. Music education in the twenty-first century. *Music Educators Journal* 84(3): 33–8.

Reimer, B. 2003a. *A philosophy of music education: Advancing the vision.* 3rd edn. Englewood Cliffs, NJ: Prentice Hall.

Reimer, B. 2003b. Response to the reviews. *Action, Criticism and Theory for Music Education* [online]. Available at: http://act.maydaygroup.org/articles/Vogt2_1.pdf [accessed 19 April 2008].

Richardson, L. 2003. Writing: A method of inquiry. *In* N.K. Denzin and Y.S. Lincoln eds. *Collecting and interpreting qualitative materials.* Thousand Oaks, CA: Sage, pp. 499–541.

Richardson, L. and Lockridge, E. 2004. *Travels with Ernest: Crossing the literary/ sociological divide.* Walnut Creek, CA: AltaMira Press.

Richardson, L. and St Pierre, E.A. 2005. Writing: A method of inquiry. *In* N.K. Denzin and Y.S. Lincoln eds. *The Sage handbook of qualitative research.* Thousand Oaks, CA: Sage, pp. 959–78.

Richardson, V. 1996. The roles of attitudes and beliefs in learning to teach. *In* J. Sikula ed. *Handbook of research on teacher education.* New York: Macmillan, pp. 102–19.

Richardson, V. 2003. Preservice teachers' beliefs. *In* J. Raths and A.C. McAninch eds. *Teacher beliefs and classroom performance: The impact of teacher education.* Greenwich, CT: IAP, pp. 1–22.

Richardson, V. and Kile, R.S. 1999. The use of videocases in teacher education. *In* M. Lundberg, B. Levin and H. Harrington eds. *Who learns from cases and how? The research base for teaching with cases.* Hillsdale, NJ: Erlbaum, pp. 121–36.

Rizvi, F. and Lingard, B. 2010. *Globalizing education policy.* New York: Routledge.

Ross, M. 1995. What's wrong with school music? *British Journal of Music Education* 12(3): 185–201.

Rubin, H.J. and Rubin, I.S. 2005. *Qualitative interviewing: The art of hearing data.* 2nd edn. Thousand Oaks, CA: Sage.

Rusinek, G. 2008. Disaffected learners and school musical culture: An opportunity for inclusion. *Research Studies in Music Education* 30(1): 9–23.

Schmidt, P. 2005. Music education as transformative practice: Creating new frameworks for learning music through a Freirian perspective. *Visions of research in music education* [online]. Available at: http://www.rider.edu/~vrme [accessed 1 April 2009].

Schön, D.A. 1987. *Educating the reflective practitioner: Toward a new design for teaching and learning in the professions.* San Francisco: Jossey-Bass.

Scott, D.B. 1990. Music and sociology for the 1990s: A changing critical perspective. *Musical Quarterly* 72(3): 385–410.

Small, C. 1977. *Music society, education: A radical examination of the prophetic function in Western, Eastern and African cultures with its impact of society and its use in education.* London: John Calder.

Small, C. 1987. *Music of the common tongue.* London: John Calder.

Small, C. 1998. *Musicking: The meanings of performing and listening.* Middletown, CT: Wesleyan University Press.

Stahl, M.W. 2004. A moment like this: American Idol and narratives of meritocracy. *In* C.J. Washburne and M. Derno eds. *Bad music: The music we love to hate.* New York: Routledge, pp. 165–85.

Stake, R.E. 1995. *The art of case study research.* Thousand Oaks, CA: Sage.

Stake, R.E. 2005. Qualitative case studies. *In* N.K. Denzin and Y.S. Lincoln eds. *The sage handbook of qualitative research.* Thousand Oaks, CA: Sage, pp. 443–66.

Swanwick, K. 1999. *Teaching music musically.* London: Routledge.

The State of Queensland 1995. Music senior syllabus. Spring Hill: Queensland Board of Senior Secondary School Studies.

The State of Queensland 2004. Senior syllabus: Music. Spring Hill: Queensland Studies Authority.

Thomson, P. 2008. Field. *In* M. Grenfell ed. *Pierre Bourdieu: Key concepts*. Durham: Acumen, pp. 67–81.

Tillema, H. and Knoll, W. 1997. Promoting student teacher instruction through conceptual change or direct instruction. *Teaching and Teacher Education* 13(6): 579–95.

Tucker, J. 1996. From performer to school music teacher: A problem of identity. *In* M. Kompf *et al.* eds. *Changing research and practice: Teachers' professionalism identities and knowledge*. London: Falmer.

Turino, T. 2008. *Music as social life: The politics of participation*. Chicago: University of Chicago Press.

Väkevä, L. 2006. Teaching popular music in Finland: What's up, what's ahead? *International Journal of Music Education* 24: 126–31.

Väkevä, L. 2012. The world well lost, found: Reality and authenticity in Green's 'New classroom pedagogy'. *In* S. Karlsen and L. Väkevä eds. *Future prospects for music education: Corroborating informal learning pedagogy*. Newcastle upon Tyne: Cambridge Scholars Publishing, pp. 23–49.

Väkevä, L. and Westerlund, H. 2007. The 'method' of democracy in music education. *Action, Criticism and Theory for Music Education* [online]. Available at: http://act.maydaygroup.org/articles/V%C3%A4kev%C3%A4_Westerlund6_4.pdf [accessed 21 April 2008].

Vaugeois, L. 2007. Social justice and music education: Claiming the space of music education as a site of postcolonial contestation. *Action, Criticism and Theory for Music Education* [online]. Available at: http://act.maydaygroup.org/articles/Vaugeois6_4.pdf [accessed 21 April 2008].

Wacquant, L. 2014a. Homines in extremis: What fighting scholars teach us about habitus. *Body and Society* 20(2): 3–17.

Wacquant, L. 2014b. Putting habitus in its place: Rejoinder to the symposium. *Body and Society* 20(2): 118–39.

Wacquant, L. 2015. For a sociology of flesh and blood. *Qualitative Sociology* 38(1): 1–11.

Westerlund, H. 2006. Garage rock bands: A future model for developing musical expertise? *International Journal of Music Education* 24: 119–25.

Woodford, P.G. 2005. *Democracy and music education: Liberalism, ethics and the politics of practice*. Bloomington: Indiana University Press.

Wright, R. 2008. Kicking the habitus: Power, culture and pedagogy in the secondary school music curriculum. *Music Education Research* 10(3): 389–402.

Index

Aboriginal communities 64
Abramo, J.M. 52
Adler, A. 61–2
aesthetic experience 26–7
agency: of students 35; of teachers 32
alienation of teachers and students 135
Allan, J. 64–8, 84
American Indians 23
Anang Ibibio people 23
'art for art's sake' 21
art music 2, 4, 21–4, 30, 85–6, 121,
    133–8, 143
artistic integrity 21
artistry, prioritisation of 2
Australian Curriculum 118

Bach, J.S. 56
Ballantyne, J. 33–4
'banking' concept of education
    (Freire) 28
Barker, P. 115–19
Barone, T. 6, 8
Barrett, M.S. 5
beliefs of music teachers see values
    and beliefs
Benedict, C. 135
Bennett, T. 59
Berlin Philharmonic 34
Blackfield State High School 88–110
Bouij, C. 24
Bourdieu, P. (and Bourdeuian analysis)
    5–8, 15–18, 21, 31, 34, 36, 47, 133, 143
Bowman, W.D. 32
Bradley, D. 32
'bumping places' (Clandinin) 142

'canon', the 2; see also musical works
capital: different forms of 18–19;
    sociological concept of 6, 18–19

Chanan, M. 23
Chiswick College 63–87, 137–41
Clandinin, D.J. 5–6, 10, 39, 142
classical music 17, 21, 32, 122, 135, 138
classroom music 41, 126–7, 137
Cochran-Smith, M. 31
communal music making 2
composers, power of 23–4
Connelly, F.M. 5
conservatism in music teaching 2–3, 32
conservatories 24
construction: of knowledge 7; of
    music-making 12
constructivist-structuralism in
    sociology 16
Cook, M. 45–62, 133–40
Creswell, J.W. 5
cultural capital 18–19; embodied,
    objectified or institutionalised 18–19;
    purposes served by 19

Debussy, C. 24
Densmore, K. 33
Denzin, N.K. 5–6
dialectical approach to music education 28
'disaffected learners' 34
doxa of music and music education 8,
    12, 15, 19–28, 133–4, 138, 141, 143

East, M. 117–19, 123, 129
elitism in music-making 12, 21–2, 25–6,
    135, 140
Elliott, D.J. 27–8, 34
Emmison, M. 59
epistemology 7
Eurocentric conceptualisation of
    music 137
exclusionary practices in the classroom
    3, 21, 25

Fenstermacher, G.D. 31
field concept 6, 17–18, 30, 133
field notes 4
Freire, P. 28
Frow, J. 59

Gale, T. 33
Gardner, H. 27–8
Gates, J.T. 32
gender stereotypes 59–62
grand narratives of music teachers 32
Green, L. 3, 25, 29, 52, 140
Gudmundsdottir, S. 5

habitus 6–8, 15–19, 30–1, 36, 133–4,
    141, 143; components of 16;
    definition of 16
Hall, Sam 63, 68–87, 134–41
Hargreaves, D.J. 30
Harrison, S.D. 60–2
hegemonic masculinity 60–2
Heidegren, C.-G. 20
hierarchy of musical activities 2, 8,
    21, 23–4

'idol' phenomenon 25
'illusio' concept 15, 19–20
Indigenous education 64–8, 75–6
individuation, biological 16
informal approaches to music and
    learning 3, 23, 29, 32, 53–4, 137–40
international students 116
interviews used for research 4

jazz 2
Jørgensen, H. 28
Juntenen, M.L. 32

Kang, I. 81–5, 137
Kingsbury, H. 22–3
Knoll, W. 31
Kodály methodology 11, 72, 85, 98
Koza, J. 23, 112–13

'labelling' of students 2, 22–3
Langer, S.K. 26
Laws, J. 88–90, 93–110, 134–9, 142–3
learning experiences 36
Levine, L.W. 24–5
Levi-Strauss, C. 24
lifelong learning 119–23
Lincoln, Y.S. 5–6
Lingard, B. 7

literacy in language and in music 108, 138
Loughran, J.J. 142
Lundberg, H. 20

McEwan, R.W. 53
Major, C. 135
Matiero, T. 31
Maton, K. 17
member checking 6
Merriam, A.P. 23
Messenger, J. 23
meta-reflection 141
Meyer, L.B. 26
Mills, C. 33–4
Mills, J. 33
Moore, R. 18–19
Murphy, M.S. 39
music education: changes in 3; as distinct
    from other academic disciplines 139
Music Education as Aesthetic Education
    (MEAE) 25–7
music teachers: basic premises about 1;
    different experience of music from
    their students 1; identity of 2;
    personal and/or professional growth
    of 140, 143; professional knowledge
    of 31–2; professional role of 12; see
    also socialisation; values and beliefs
Musical Futures programme 29, 32
musical styles 2
musical works, study of 2, 139
'musicality' 23
'musicianism' 31
'musicianship' 28, 134, 136
'musicing' 27

narrative inquiry 4–9, 39
Nettl, B. 22, 24
Noddings, N. 109
notation, musical 134–6

'objective' knowledge 7
observation as part of research 4
Ollererenshaw, J.A. 5

Palmer, B. 135
Parker, A. 60
participatory music-making 22, 138–9;
    by students outside the classroom 11
Penderecki, K. 122
Philpott, C. 2, 32
'plots' showing linkages within data 5
Plummer, D. 60

Polkinghorne, D.E. 5
polyvocal conversation 8
popular music 2, 25, 29, 35, 126, 138, 140
positionality of the researcher 7
'prac' (practical work) 11, 40–1, 120–1
praxial philosophy of music education 25, 27–8, 34
preparation for tertiary music studies 1, 133, 135
'presentational' music-making 22
procedural knowledge 27
professionalism in music 23

Queensland 37–40, 47, 51, 55, 72, 104, 135–8

recursive approach to data generation 5
reflective dialogue 142–3
'reflex reflexivity' (Bourdieu) 7
reflexivity: of practitioners 10; of researchers 7
Regelski, T.A. 31
Reimer, B. 26–7
relational sociology 11–20, 133
repertoire, choice of 125–7, 137
research design for study of music teachers 5–7
restricted production, field of 21
Richardson, L. 5–6
Richardson, V. 30–1
Rizvi, F. 7
Rosiek, J. 6
Ross, M. 32–3
Rusinek, G. 34–5

'sacralisation' of music 24
St Mark's College 43–62, 140
St Pierre, E.A. 5–6
Schönberg, A. 22, 24, 125–6
schooling 15, 17
Seaview High School 111–29
'sheep and goats' approach to music education 33
Small, C. 2, 8, 12, 24, 27, 59

social capital 18, 47
social justice 40
socialisation: of music teachers 1–3, 30–2; primary 19
sociology of education 15–16; *see also* relational sociology
specialisation in music 23
Stauffer, S.L. 5
story-telling 10
Stravinsky, I. 125–6
streaming 119
structuralist-constructivism in sociology 16
subfields, artistic 21
Swanwick, K. 27
symphony concert tradition 24–5

talent seen as a prerequisite for music-making 22–9, 33–5, 138
teacher-centred pedagogy 140
teacher training 11, 31, 134–5
technique (musical), importance of 121, 136–7
Tillema, H. 31
traditions of music-making and music education 3, 12, 24–5, 32
triangulation 5–6
Tucker, J. 35

values and beliefs of music teachers 3–4, 8, 10, 12, 30–3, 133, 135, 140, 143
vocational education and training (VET) 41

Wacquant, L. 16–17
Westerlund, H. 28, 32
Western music-making 1–2, 4, 7–8, 12, 21–7, 30, 32, 85–6, 121, 133–8, 143
Westvall, M. 31
whole-class singing 138
whole-school culture 57–62
Wood, J. 111–15, 119–29, 133–40
Woodford, P.G. 26
world music 27, 101, 127
Wright, R. 35

Taylor & Francis eBooks

Helping you to choose the right eBooks for your Library

Add Routledge titles to your library's digital collection today. Taylor and Francis ebooks contains over 50,000 titles in the Humanities, Social Sciences, Behavioural Sciences, Built Environment and Law.

Choose from a range of subject packages or create your own!

Benefits for you

>> Free MARC records
>> COUNTER-compliant usage statistics
>> Flexible purchase and pricing options
>> All titles DRM-free.

REQUEST YOUR **FREE** INSTITUTIONAL TRIAL TODAY

Free Trials Available
We offer free trials to qualifying academic, corporate and government customers.

Benefits for your user

>> Off-site, anytime access via Athens or referring URL
>> Print or copy pages or chapters
>> Full content search
>> Bookmark, highlight and annotate text
>> Access to thousands of pages of quality research at the click of a button.

eCollections – Choose from over 30 subject eCollections, including:

Archaeology	Language Learning
Architecture	Law
Asian Studies	Literature
Business & Management	Media & Communication
Classical Studies	Middle East Studies
Construction	Music
Creative & Media Arts	Philosophy
Criminology & Criminal Justice	Planning
Economics	Politics
Education	Psychology & Mental Health
Energy	Religion
Engineering	Security
English Language & Linguistics	Social Work
Environment & Sustainability	Sociology
Geography	Sport
Health Studies	Theatre & Performance
History	Tourism, Hospitality & Events

For more information, pricing enquiries or to order a free trial, please contact your local sales team: **www.tandfebooks.com/page/sales**

Routledge
Taylor & Francis Group

The home of
Routledge books

www.tandfebooks.com